The Corporation and the Campus

The Corporation and the Campus

Edited by Robert H. Connery

Published for
The Academy of Political Science
Columbia University
by

PRAEGER PUBLISHERS

New York • Washington • London

PRAEGER PUBLISHERS

111 Fourth Avenue, New York, N. Y. 10003, U.S.A.
5, Cromwell Place, London S. W. 7, England

Published in the United States of America in 1970
by Praeger Publishers, Inc.

© 1970 by The Academy of Political Science

Library of Congress Catalog Card Number: 79-106035

Printed in the United States of America

Most of the papers in *The Corporation and the Campus* were delivered
at a conference co-sponsored by the Academy of Political Science and
the Council for Financial Aid to Education at the New York Hilton on
November 6, 1969. The conference and this volume were made possible by a grant from the Alfred P. Sloan Foundation.

Contents

Preface

The press has made everyone aware of student unrest, but the future of the colleges and universities in America may depend on less dramatic issues. Accelerating enrollment, a wider range of activities, and the admission of more students from minority groups, as well as inflation and the complex problems arising from growth and social change, make the problem of finance crucial to the future of higher education.

Higher levels of technical skill for more people than ever before are needed by American industry. Consequently the continuation and expansion of higher education is basic to the self-interest of industry. This has led executives of some of the largest corporations in this country advocate massive support of the colleges and universities. Voluntary support by individuals and by business has always been an important part in the financing of higher education, but this support must increase if the financial needs are to be met.

The Academy of Political Science and the Council for Financial Aid to Education jointly sponsored a conference in New York City in November 1969 to bring together educational leaders, corporation executives, and spokesmen for minority groups, to examine the scope of the problems in higher education that will have to be faced in the coming decade. Papers given at that conference, together with others prepared especially for this volume, are published here. An attempt has been made to project the financial needs of higher education, possible sources of funds from student charges and the government, as well as the amount of voluntary support that will be required.

The Academy of Political Science, an independent corporation with headquarters on the Columbia University campus, serves as a forum for the discussion of public policy questions. While it takes no official position on these questions, it hopes, through its conferences and publications, to present in an objective and scholarly manner various points of view.

The Council for Financial Aid to Education, a nonprofit service organization, was established in 1952, largely through the efforts of three prominent businessmen: Frank W. Abrams, the late Irving S. Olds, and Alfred P. Sloan, Jr. It was supported originally by four major foundations: the Carnegie Corporation of New York, the Ford Foundation, the Rockefeller Foundation, and the Alfred P. Sloan Foundation. It is now financed by over two hundred corporations.

The Council's purpose is to promote a deeper understanding of the importance of higher education and to stimulate the widest possible voluntary support of colleges and universities, especially by business. It encourages, but neither solicits nor disburses, funds for higher education. Its unique program consists of studies in educational philanthropy, both business- and college-oriented; a national public service advertising campaign utilizing the familiar theme "Give to the college of your choice"; informational publications to broaden the base of college support; a consultation service for businesses on aid-to-education programs; symposiums for corporation officers and college administrators; and a national series of key city meetings for top-echelon business executives.

The Council and the Academy are grateful to the Alfred P. Sloan Foundation for the financial support that made the conference and this volume possible, and to the presiding officers, commentators, and the five hundred persons attending the conference.

ROBERT H. CONNERY
President of the Academy

Contributors

NORMAN P. AUBURN is president of the University of Akron.

ROGER M. BLOUGH, former chairman of the board of directors and chief executive officer, U.S. Steel Corporation, is presently chairman of the board of the Council for Financial aid to Education.

HOWARD R. BOWEN, chairman of the department of economics at the Claremont Graduate School, has been president of Grinnell College and of the University of Iowa.

KINGMAN BREWSTER is president of Yale University.

ROBERT H. CONNERY is professor of government in Columbia University and president of the Academy of Political Science.

CHARLES V. HAMILTON, professor of government in Columbia University, is coauthor of *Black Power: The Politics of Liberation in America.*

JAMES M. HESTER is president of New York University.

EDGAR F. KAISER is chairman of the board and chief executive officer of Kaiser Industries Corporation.

J. R. KILLIAN, JR., is chairman of the corporation, Massachusetts Institute of Technology.

WILLIAM F. MAY is chairman of the board and president of the American Can Company.

CHARLES B. McCOY is president of E. I. du Pont de Nemours & Company, Inc.

JOHN D. MILLETT, chancellor of the Ohio Board of Regents and former president of Miami University in Oxford, Ohio, has served as executive director of the Commission on Financing Higher Education.

JAMES F. OATES, JR., is chairman of the board and chief executive officer of the Equitable Life Assurance Society of the United States.

JUNE O'NEILL is a research associate at the Brookings Institution.

CONTRIBUTORS

ALICE M. RIVLIN, senior fellow of the Brookings Institution, is the author of *The Role of the Federal Government in Financing Higher Education.*

HAYDEN W. SMITH is vice president for research of the Council for Financial Aid to Education.

W. CLARKE WESCOE, former chancellor of the University of Kansas, is vice president for medical affairs of the Sterling Drug Company, Inc.

FRANKLIN H. WILLIAMS has served as United States Ambassador to Ghana and as director of the Urban Center at Columbia University.

JOSEPH C. WILSON is chairman and chief executive officer of the Xerox Corporation.

ROBERT C. WOOD, former undersecretary of the Department of Housing and Urban Development, is director of the M.I.T.-Harvard Urban Studies Center.

HARRIET A. ZUCKERMAN is a member of the department of sociology at Columbia University.

The Urban Crisis

ROBERT C. WOOD

HARRIET A. ZUCKERMAN

At a time when many doubt whether American universities can save themselves, it seems gratuitous to ask if they can save American cities. As effective, functioning institutions, universities appear too often these days in a shambles—at least as compared to their peaceful state of a decade ago. Colleges and universities are now attacked by students and faculty, by legislators, and by members of the communities in which they are located. Many of those privately endowed are near financial collapse.

Therefore, the university seems an unlikely savior of the city, in a time when, finally, the urban crisis is no longer a matter for dispute, even though the character of the crisis may still be debatable. Some believe that the physical blight and decay of the cities, pollution, crime, and racial tensions are part of a more general crisis in American society. Others are more modest in their analysis; they concentrate on the effects that high levels of congestion, density, and interaction have on human psychology and biology. But whatever the nature of urban difficulties—ubiquitous and obvious, subtle and complex—the needs of the American city are substantial. And, the capabilities of the universities to meet these needs are limited.

Given the contrast of a poor state of readiness on the part of universities and a compelling need for reform and relief of cities, it may be suggested that skepticism is a fitting response to claims that universities will save the cities. Indeed, there has been a long history of conflict between the two. Yet there are critical, if modest, services

that universities can perform for cities that would be of mutual benefit. If cities and universities are to fare well in the future, coordinated change and strengthening will be required.

Conflicts Between Town and Gown

The traditional division of the university and the community into
"town and gown" suggests that long-lived strains between them may
militate against satisfactory joint efforts to solve the urban crisis. It
is worthwhile to examine some sources of these conflicts for the cues
they give to fundamental, enduring tensions between universities and
their communities. The first clearly recorded "collisions" occurred in
1214 when, according to the historian of universities, Hastings
Rashdall, the bell of St. Mary's at Oxford summoned "the gownsmen
to do battle with the town."[1]

Both sides then had reason to take offense. The scholars resented the
physical violence done them by townsmen, charging that students
were regularly tormented. These fights culminated in the brawl on
St. Scholastica feast day. As Anthony à Wood described it, "Some
twenty Inns or Halls were pillaged. Scholars were killed or wounded;
their eatables and drinkables plundered; their books torn to pieces;
the Halls themselves fired."[2]

Townsmen had legitimate grievances, too. In particular they com-
plained about the growing control by the university not only over
the scholars, but over laymen as well. University authority had become so oppressive that Parliament discussed how town burghers
might be protected from the chancellors. Cambridge and Oxford
claimed the right to control their own members, and to ensure their
autonomy they attempted to extend their control to all other persons
in their local environment. At the same time, they sought relief from
taxation and other fiscal and civic liabilities. The present reluctance
to use local police in university disturbances is both an echo of traditional aversion to the use of force on the campus and of a continuing
sense that university autonomy is threatened by civil authority.

Jurisdictional matters aside, townsmen also found the behavior of
students and scholars loutish, vulgar, and rowdy. Thus the claim of
one Parisian official in 1269 that scholars "by day and night atro-

---

[1] Hastings Rashdall, *The Universities of Europe in the Middle Ages*, Vol. 2 (Oxford, 1895), 686.
[2] *Ibid.*, 405.

ciously wound and slay many, carry off women, ravish virgins, break into houses," and commit "over and over again robberies and many other enormities hateful to God."[3] This account of thirteenth-century students makes the actions of students today seem tame.

To conflicts over jurisdiction and comportment could be added competition between town and gown for land—territoriality and turf. In medieval times areas set aside for the colleges were invaded by townspeople who believed the universities' privileges excessive. Then as now surrounding neighborhoods were pressed by university needs, and people were displaced to make room for college buildings.

Finally, tensions were often generated by the relatively aristocratic or clerical cast of the university in contrast to the plebian style of residents of the community. It is reported that the early democracy of student recruitment in medieval times later gave way to entrance on the basis of ability to pay. Indeed, students in the first private American universities, by and large, were well-to-do and continued to be so until recent times. Townsmen often believed that university graduates did not deserve their good fortune. This resentment was combined with a sense of inferiority *vis à vis* university members.

At various times, then, and in various places, conflicts between town and gown were rooted in competition for sovereignty and for land, the mutual disregard of students and their neighbors, and the "class" conflict between university and town. These have often combined to make cooperation between universities and communities difficult indeed.

Changes in the Relations Between Town and Gown

Dubious beginnings give way to better prospects now. Conflicts between universities and their communities are far from over, but the promise of effective cooperation between them has been improved since World War II. Although conflicts with local residents have continued, some universities have joined with communities in producing better community services, housing, and schools. For one thing, the battle over sovereignty has quieted as the division of authority between community and university has been regularized. More concretely, lines of jurisdiction between the two have been increasingly

[3] *Ibid.*, 682.

clarified, and it is only on occasions such as students' attacks on the universities that it is not entirely clear whether universities will maintain the right to discipline or whether the community has a higher authority in such matters. In any case, the two in this situation have been allied rather than in conflict.

On the issue of turf, the relatively polarized camps of the past are no longer as neatly divided as they once were. Universities are beginning to take more responsibility for people in their vicinity displaced by expansion. Although the reality of shrinking amounts of free space in cities helps to maintain competition between urban universities and their neighbors, and even to intensify it, the problem this has created has led to further collaboration between them.

Finally, communities surrounding universities are apparently less hostile to students than they once were, even though they are still ambivalent. The symbol of long hair and the fact of radical political action still grate on some public nerves, but students have become advocates within the university for community rights, and larger numbers also engage in community service. At least the level of contentions has moved beyond the panty raid and the hot rod.

Class antagonisms between universities and their environing areas once so visible are also fading. Recruitment of students from less-advantaged social groups, the rising level of educational attainment among the population, and the transformation of university faculties from the aristocratic model to a cosmopolitan one contribute to this change. This does not mean that conflict based on class differentials no longer exists, but a relatively uneducated community is not pitted against the upper-class university to the same degree as before. One vestige of class antagonisms probably remains. The frequent and sometimes violent clashes between students and local police surely reflect old resentments. Students feel that the police are lower-class bullies, and the police, in turn, are deeply antagonized by "spoiled" middle-class students who do not deserve the free ride of a college education.

Even if these imperfections are acknowledged, however, change has left the relations between universities and communities in a somewhat better, if more complicated, state than they were in the past. It is clear that universities and communities need not be combatants on every front, but there are reasons for continued competition between them—for space, in particular—which good intentions on both sides are not apt to remove.

Contemporary University Contributions

Universities have undergone changes in the last decades that increase their chances of effectively contributing to the solution of urban difficulties. For one thing, the social sciences are developing some expertness in dealing with practical problems. For another, many faculty members have become interested in dealing with these problems. Finally, universities have willy-nilly become involved in community problems and have a stake in their solution.

There is, as most scholars of urban life admit, little in the way of systematized knowledge about urban phenomena which would provide the base for practical action, and it would be absurd to expect anything like the success scientists have had in marshalling knowledge for the solution of defense and space problems. Nevertheless, the social sciences continue to become more empirical and policy-oriented, and some show promise for helping to implement policy decisions. Changes in the professorial role complement this development. Since World War II, professors have become more interested in extramural projects, particularly those which will have socially useful outcomes and which promise to expand intellectual competence. The old idea of the professor whose concerns are strictly confined to the ivory tower has given way to a new academic ethos which permits professorial involvement in a variety of projects without the loss of collegial approval. As a consequence, government, business, and labor groups are receiving more expert advice than ever before, and professors, in turn, are discouraged from being mere academics.

Just as the activities of professors have become more heterogeneous, so also have the functions of the university, though more by chance than by design. Often without serious consideration, universities have accepted a variety of missions which have been thrust upon them. In part, the success of academics in wartime activities—in the Office of Strategic Services, the Manhattan Project, and in the development of radar—led to their being asked to take on new tasks; but success is not the only reason. Other social agencies—schools, housing authorities, and cultural institutions—have not been successful in solving urban problems. Therefore, there has been a demand for aid from the universities. Changes in the role of universities and faculty since the war have altered the prospects for new university knowledge in helping solve the urban crisis. Like any organization, a university has a basic interest in its environment—the space in which its members live and work. Lately, for more and more universities, that environment has become threatened by change and decay in land use and function.

Universities located in rural areas, as many land-grant colleges were, and the many which were originally established in middle-class sections of the cities did not face these problems until recently —and a limited number do not face them now. But most urban universities find they must take an interest in their local environments not only out of compassion and conscience but out of self-interest. Urban universities located in or near slums find it difficult to attract able faculty and students.[4] Moreover, some observers of the university scene attribute student unrest not only to the poor university organization but also to dissatisfaction with urban life. Increasingly, then, universities have come to have a stake in improving their local environments, a fact possibly first appreciated by the University of Chicago, which had a major role in reconstructing the Hyde Park-Kenwood area. The same sort of motivations have guided the University of Pennsylvania's reclamation of its decaying neighborhood and the ambitious housing programs of the Massachusetts Institute of Technology and Harvard. As a consequence, the inevitable strains between universities and communities have diminished in some cases, but in others they have deepened the old suspicions between the two. The changing relations between university and community, the continuing role of curiosity sensitized by considerations of domestic priorities, and the practical compulsion of organizational maintenance suggest that the gown is more disposed than it once was to join with the town in dealing with the urban crisis. The real question remains: What can the university do that will be effective and worthwhile but will not interfere with its primary responsibility?

A Division of Labor Among Universities

If town and gown are not destined to continuous confrontation, neither are they equipped to be in continuous collaboration. The beginning of wisdom about the academic role in the urban crisis is that

---

[4] Medieval Oxford did not escape the polutions of an urban location either. Things became so bad in the fourteenth century that a Royal letter, written probably on university instigation, was sent to the sheriff complaining, " 'the air is so corrupted and infected' by the filth in the streets 'that an abominable loathing' (or perhaps 'ague') is 'diffused among the aforesaid Masters and scholars,' a state of things aggravated by the practice of "' burning fat . . . before their houses.'" Ibid., 389.

the university in general cannot cure all urban ills, and universities in particular vary widely in the assignments that each might undertake. Some can do much, many can do something, and some can do only little.

A first step toward understanding how universities can help solve urban problems is to match types of universities with types of tasks. Too often stressing their deep dissatisfaction with the quality of urban life, social critics have cast all universities into the same mold by calling on them as a group to redirect their efforts toward social action: altering housing policy, eliminating racial inequities, and, not least important, solving the problems of the cities. The sense of urgency ought not to be lost, but it should be accompanied by an effort to think specifically about the unique abilities of different kinds of universities for dealing with the problem at hand. Granting that distinctions have been blurred in recent years, the classical categories of public, private, and denominational institutions still give clues as to appropriate assignments.

In the division of labor which is most apt to be effective, publicly sponsored institutions have responsibility for the greater share of urban scholarship and urban research, though not all of it. Their resources are greater and their financing more secure than those of all but a handful of private universities. An even more compelling reason for their greater responsibility is their capacity to identify with state and local governments on the firing line of urban problems. Nevertheless, private universities have their own contributions to make. Typically, they have a greater measure of flexibility and freedom and in certain circumstances find it easier to undertake controversial programs that involve direct observation and evaluation of experimental public programs. The M.I.T.-Harvard Joint Center for Urban Studies' assessments of public programs, for example, have been controversial and required consideration and response on the part of policymakers. More important, private universities may undertake long lead-time research in urban affairs with a less-immediate sense of obligation to report their utility. This diversity of educational institutions by kind and place in the United States is an advantage in urban studies and suggests a division of labor that should be exploited.

Universities are also differentiated according to size and according to the quality of their faculties, students, and administrators. Small institutions obviously cannot undertake the kind of big-scale operation in urban research that their larger colleagues can. Their resources are limited, and also the balance of activities in small institutions can more easily be thrown askew by the introduction of a single large-scale program. Candid recognition of differences in the quality of intellectual resources that different institutions can mobilize is also in order. A community college can carry out tasks that a prestigious national university cannot and vice versa. Remedial education for disadvantaged students is probably no more effectively provided by professorial members of the American Philosophical Society or the National Academy of Sciences than by some of their able but less-well-known colleagues in community colleges. This matter calls to mind the remark made by an able college freshman who happened to be taking elementary physics with a Nobel laureate. When asked how the course was going, he answered somewhat ruefully, "It's like using a very big steam shovel to dig a very little hole." Variations in academic capacity now need to be systematically discussed and acknowledged as part of the process of timely and effective aid by the university.

To differences among academic institutions should be added differences among communities as part of the process of devising an effective division of labor. American universities relate to a spectrum of constituencies, clientele, and communities scattered across the urban scene. Harvard University is a useful illustration. It is, of course, situated in a small city, but Harvard's historic role in American society and her present contributions to science, scholarship, and government are scarcely affected by her precise geographical location. Harvard has a national and world constituency, not a local one. The same is true in differing degrees for every great university. The interests and capabilities of the California Institute of Technology are not circumscribed by Pasadena; they extend across the country and beyond. Some may not be accustomed to this view inasmuch as the United States has never had a national university. No Frenchman would seriously suggest that the Sorbonne's main job is to tend to the needs of Paris, and no Englishman thinks of Oxford and Cambridge as suburban institutions.

By contrast, many other colleges and universities are oriented primarily to meeting the needs of their local communities. This observation is not to relieve the great universities of responsibility to their immediate surroundings but instead to help sort out which universities ought to be contributing what services to whom.

This characterization of universities has implications for financing as well. If it is the case that Harvard's prime contributions are national and that the same is true for the University of Chicago, or the California Institute of Technology, then it follows that Cambridge, Chicago, and Pasadena should not foot all the bills, through tax exemptions, for these institutions. Instead, the major recipients of the services of the great universities, government and business, should pay for them, at least in large measure. Under the present system of tax exemptions, university communities can be fiscally penalized (though they benefit in other respects, to be sure). For example, Cambridge pays for what Washington gets, and Harvard and the Massachusetts Institute of Technology payments in lieu of local taxes do in fact acknowledge this situation in Cambridge and Boston. The federal government has gone some distance toward this by concentrating federal research moneys in the great national universities.

The implications of this distinction between national and local universities for participation in dealing with the urban crisis are fairly clear. National universities are best equipped to direct their efforts to large-scale programs, those requiring multiple and highly skilled competences, those involving problems of coordination among disciplines and professional schools, and those which might be thought of as fundamental rather than applied research. They need not attend primarily to the problems which are more or less idiosyncratic to a particular region or location. This means that localities should perhaps be asked to pay, through university financing, for the tailoring of general solutions to meet their specific needs, but they should not be asked to finance the development of major programs. These require more and different support from business corporations, foundations, and the federal government. Differentiation and the division of labor among universities are principles for understanding how the university comes to work with the city.

University Action

A special principle, granted differentiation by type, is limitation by general institutional competence. Although one is apt to think that there is no societal problem for which some expertise is irrelevant, the fact is that universities do some things well and others things poorly. Their members are not equally competent to deal with every social problem, nor do they have resources to deal with them all. With this perspective on the capacities of universities, the sort of activities that are inappropriate and appropriate for them to undertake can be indicated.

Universities are not apt to substitute effectively for municipal and state authorities which must take prime responsibility for providing public services. Because the problems are so compelling, universities are often called upon to relieve economic distress in their communities, to fill the breach for inadequate public housing, to provide for more equitable administration of justice, and to improve primary and secondary education. University response to these problems is not likely to be adequate, and providing minimal relief has the unwanted consequence of decreasing the chances of reform in public services. On the other hand, there are special circumstances under which universities might be especially equipped to deal with all of these problems.

Universities run a risk when they enter into local political activities in such a way as to upset local power constellations. Universities cannot adequately or legitimately assume responsibility for political acts. If they corporately engage in local politics, they run the risk of paying a high price for doing so. Since the only redress politicians have against universities involve limitations of autonomy and support, it is in these two areas that universities will suffer most. Universities cannot insist on immunity from public pressure if they enter the political arena, and they cannot insist on continued financing if they engage in politics contrary to those who vote for them.

Universities are better able to deal with matters to which expertise is relevant and available. On these grounds, they need to devise means for assessing which claims on them are appropriate and which are not. Some question, for example, the usefulness of university participation in the ghetto-entrepreneurship program when faculties of business schools need to learn more than they know now about ghetto economics. At the same time, no one questions the necessity for studies to increase knowledge of these and related matters. Similarly, lending university prestige to haphazard and "instant" evaluation of urban programs jeopardizes the universities and does not produce effective and useful assessments.

These are merely caveats. They are not intended to say that the university should retreat from involvement in the effort to solve urban problems. On the contrary, there is an unmistakable trend toward increasing university engagement in societal matters of all sorts. This trend toward greater involvement cannot be attributed only to the thrusting of new responsibilities onto universities. Carl Kaysen is quite right in observing that universities have, since the forties, reached out for new activities not because they are conscience-stricken but because these new activities have an intellectual justification and are of interest to university faculties.[5] Kaysen's remarks alert one to the principle on which such involvements should be assessed. Universities are organized primarily for the production and transmission of knowledge, and while this sounds excessively abstract and high-minded, it does provide a rough criterion for judging which kinds of involvements make the most sense. In general, universities do best by readily accepting those tasks which are consistent with this principle and which relate them symbiotically to their communities, local and national.

University health services provide a model for symbiotic relations between university and community. Medical schools depend for high quality on a wide variety of patients best supplied by large city populations. University hospitals need numerous local residents to support the various services they offer, and they depend for clinical staffing on a large base of practicing physicians located nearby. In turn, residents of university communities are apt to receive better medical attention than they would get at local hospitals and health stations. The mutual benefits derived by universities and communities from medical education and services are not vitiated by the many and justified complaints about the way the system actually works and the fact that many physicians themselves are unhappy about the quality of services they provide. But problems that conceivably can be solved by more effective management do not falsify the main point. There are a variety of community-related activities which benefit both universities and communities and make their relations symbiotic. And it is these which are appropriate for universities. Some activities which use the distinctive capacities of universities and which benefit communities include:

• The provision of manpower trained to meet national and local community needs for professional services and equipped to deal with distinctly urban problems. This does not mean that there should be at every university a department of urban studies or a center for urban affairs. There is no discipline which falls into that rubric

[5] Carl Kaysen, "Dialogue of the Governance of Universities—I," *Daedalus* 98 (Fall 1969), 1,038.

which has academic legitimacy. As a consequence, urban departments in universities are apt to be an assortment of scholars—econo-
mists, sociologists, engineers, anthropologists, and historians—who
collectively look like members of a discipline but fail to provide an
integrated approach to urban studies. Instead there probably should
be something like urban weighting of curricula. This would involve
the representation of urban interests in most departments and professional schools, and would provide for intensive training in
urban studies without threatening the autonomy of each of these
groups. Urban institutions should have a greater urban weighting
of curricula than the traditional land-grant institutions which have
their own emphasis on agricultural research and service. This is a
start at least in producing students sensitized to urban problems and
educated to some degree to see them in perspective. It is by no means
the whole answer.

• The development of prototype housing, schools, hospitals, or
systems of transportation. Professional schools should find it both
challenging and well within the activities they consider appropriate
to design and bring to fruition models of the very best solutions to
public problems. Many universities have operated primary and secondary schools designed as laboratories for educational research and
educational training. The Lab School at Chicago and Hunter College's Elementary School have served these purposes and achieved
some success in the process. The building of prototype housing is less
common but equally desirable both for the training of university
architects and the development of better and less-costly dwellings.
There is no need to sketch out the idea of prototypes any further except to underline the necessity for experimenting with what the
most competent academic judgment considers excellent.

• The provision of professional and technical assistance to groups
—officially constituted and otherwise—undertaking the solution of
specific urban problems. This will help to bridge the gap between
academic knowledge and practical realities and, hopefully, to enhance the former by dealing with the latter. In due course, universities' capacities to produce trained manpower should also improve.

• The conduct of basic research of several kinds—traditionally
sanctioned fundamental research on urban problems, the serious
evaluation of urban programs and applied research designed to answer questions of special concern to local and federal authorities. The
first two types of investigation are reasonably familiar and need no

further comment. The last, however, provides interesting opportunities for concrete improvements in the urban condition. One form this research has already taken is the establishment of "urban observatories" designed to investigate problems selected jointly by responsible city officials and urban researchers and to provide linkages between universities and city governments. Urban observatories seem to work best in places where the university is oriented toward the local community and officialdom receptive to new ideas. They have great potential for comparative work—simultaneous investigation and report on the same urban problems and programs as they affect different communities.

This research costs money, indeed considerable amounts, but it may soon become available. The President's Committee on Urban Housing recommends, for example, that $100 million be spent on urban research by 1972, but that is no great sum compared to the total federal research and development budget which is now running between $15 and $20 billion. More support should be forthcoming from the private sector, and some bootlegging of urban research under other names—like health, public safety, and education—will have to occur. Such was the early history of research in oceanography, and the same strategy will be needed for achieving initial funding.

These simple proposals and the view of American universities' varying capacities which underlie them are not intended to satisfy any one of the main schools of thought on the role of universities in solving social problems. Those holding a conservative position on academic functions will, no doubt, think these proposals represent one more instance of the subversion of the university. Others who see the university as an instrument for the achievement of radical social change will find them eclectic, inadequate, and overly concerned with the survival of the university in its present form. The principle guiding these observations ought by now to be clear: universities help society best by redirecting their own energies and programs, not by reshaping themselves to fit some new and foreign image. One can and should invoke the civilizing values of the university in supporting its cause, but these are not its only justification. If any progress is to be made in dealing with the complicated problems that society faces, universities should not be deflected from their traditional goals. It is tempting to commit all universities to the task of trying to make urban life more bearable, but that temptation must be resisted. And by resisting the temptation to undertake everything, they may be free to do something. The sort of help they are best equipped to provide will not immediately produce what cities urgently need. Asking this much of universities, and no more, however, will help them to meet their prime responsibilities, and in the process to train new generations sufficiently sensitive to the quality of life that they will cease to be part of the problem and begin to contribute to the solution.

Minority Groups

CHARLES V. HAMILTON

During the first four months of 1969, students demanded "black studies" programs at approximately 140 colleges and universities, according to a report of the American Council on Education.[1] These demands have accelerated since the death of Dr. Martin Luther King, Jr., in Memphis on April 4, 1968, and they have reflected the growing concern of minority groups generally for a more equitable share of the benefits from the established institutions in the society—public and private, government, and private industry.

One should not be surprised that universities as well as other agencies have been targets of demands. Throughout the 1960s, black students played an important role in the overall civil rights struggle. In the early years (1960-1966), the black student activists concentrated their efforts on off-campus activities, public accommodations, and voter-registration, primarily in the South. In recent years, however, demands have focused more on campus targets and more in the North. Earlier, many young activists felt the best policy was to leave school and "go work in the community," but in the last three to four years, the nation has witnessed the development of the attitude that what was needed was the acquisition of education and skills from the university, and "the struggle" included staying in school and trying to make the universitites "more relevant" to the needs and requirements of black students.

[1] New York *Times*, May 15, 1969.

Thus, it was somewhat inevitable that various kinds of black-student organizations would develop on campuses to push for changes in the curriculum, for more black students and black faculty, and for greater involvement of the university in the development of black and Puerto Rican communities. These demands represent a commitment to education. Unlike earlier students who saw their educational experience as essentially useless and thus dropped out, black students now recognize that the university *can* be a vital resource in community development. In the same way that new groups are demanding more from local boards of education, labor unions, welfare agencies, churches, private industry, and various levels of government, so new minority student groups are demanding that the universities reexamine their programs and respond with more enlightened programs. Therefore, while the university is coming under attack in much the same way and for many of the same reasons as other institutions, there is an important consideration to be dealt with concerning higher education in this regard.

This consideration relates to the challenge that black students' demands make on the traditional role of the university in the United States. In some societies, particularly the new nations of the mid-twentieth century, the university is seen as a logical place for ferment and as a catalyst for social change. Many expect the university to graduate new elite groups who will in some way overturn the established, traditional authorities. These societies are undergoing rapid change; they are caught up in the process of political modernization. Students look to their professors and to themselves for not only the technical but the ideological tools to mount and to maintain this new thrust. But that is not the case in the United States. The university in this country, notwithstanding its stated ideal of being a place of free and open inquiry, has been a force for maintenance of societal status quo. Indeed, it has served as a gatekeeper through which one passed in his striving for individual upward mobility. As the economic situation developed in this country, access to power and wealth and higher occupational status became more and more determined by a "college education"—certainly not entirely, but more and more.

Even if employment opportunities were equal, many black people would be unable to accept the offers, because they would not have the technical skills required. Many of those skills were obtainable in college, but, as Professor Immanuel Wallerstein commented:

It is thus that, in the struggle to change the ethnic distribution of rewards, the university's policies on admissions and examinations become a critical arena. Lower ethnic groups receive poorer education in the primary and secondary schools because they are of lower social status. When the education provided is separate (de facto or de jure), it is geared to a different cultural system, and consequently it prepares the student less well for success in the testing system of the top-ranking university. Hence the rigid enforcement of objective standards tends to result in maintaining the existing ethnic allocation of rewards in the society.[2]

Many universities have increased their enrollment of black students. But the black students have not felt that those universities have done nearly enough about either changing their orientation toward the new students or toward changing conditions which would make for a more equitable society. They believe that the university has merely enrolled a few more black students in order to prepare them, as individuals, for a few slots higher up on the occupational ladder. They want greater changes than that. They talk of the university's being "relevant" to the needs of the black community, and they have in mind the university as a place where not just a few minority students come and graduate and move up and out, but where new ideas and techniques are developed for the political and economic benefit of the total black community. In other words, they look to the university, naively or not, as a beginning place for social reform or "revolution."

They see the present university system as a protector of the existing normative values and institutional structures of society, and they want the university to play a different role, to become a place that is, at least, a place of conflict with "white racist America." Otherwise, given their commitment to social change, they feel they are wasting their time. They are aware that they can acquire certain skills as engineers, doctors, architects, accountants, lawyers, teachers, physicists, and so on, but they constantly demand that they be taught how to mobilize these skills and other black people for the political-economic development of the black community. Their emphasis is on education for social action, and they feel they are betraying the black community unless they acquire this knowledge. Their orientation is toward "group" development, while they perceive the uni-

[2] Immanuel Wallerstein, *University in Turmoil: The Politics of Change* (New York, 1969), 44-45.

18 | CHARLES V. HAMILTON

versity as geared toward their "individual" upward mobility. This clash between two principles of legitimacy (individual and collective) is not an unfamiliar one to students of political modernization in developing societies.[3]

Professors Lipset and Altbach have observed the difference in university roles in developing and developed societies:

> In the developing countries, there is an intrinsic conflict between the university and the society, thereby creating a fertile ground for student political awareness and participation. The university, as one of the primary modernizing elements in largely traditional societies, necessarily finds itself opposed to other elements in its society, and must often fight to protect its values and orientation. Students are often involved in these conflicts and are key protectors of the modern orientation of the university. . . . In the developed nations, on the other hand, no such conflict exists. The university is a carrier of the traditions of the society, as well as a training agency for necessary technical skills. It is a participant in a continuing modernizing development, rather than in the vanguard of such development. University students are not called upon to protect the values of their institutions against societal encroachments. In most cases, they are merely asked to gain the qualifications necessary for a useful role in a technological society.[4]

This is an especially meaningful observation inasmuch as many black students use the analogy of the black community as a colonized society, as one undergoing development and attempting to throw off the traditional forces that rule that community in much the same way as colonies of Africa were, and are, ruled. Perhaps it is an unreasonable demand to make on American universities, but it is one on the minds and in many of the proposals of black students today. When they talk of a relevant black studies program, many have in mind some notion of this activist, challenging role, not only a program that will speak to black identity and to black culture.

It may well be that the American universities are incapable of such a role precisely because most of the professors, administrators, trustees, financial supporters, and alumni *are* committed to the preservation of the existing normative and institutional arrangements.

---

[3] See David E. Apter, *The Politics of Modernization* (Chicago, 1965).
[4] Seymour Martin Lipset and Philip G. Altbach, "Student Politics and Higher Education in the United States," in *Student Politics*, ed. Seymour Martin Lipset (New York, 1967), 242.

Likewise, it is an open question whether American universities *can* take the lead in changing the society in such a manner. And some surely would ask, Should they? At any rate, the *political* demands for *academic* relevancy raise these sorts of questions.

The Demand-Makers

It is useful to look at some data on black student activists gathered from fifteen colleges and universities across the country. Questionnaires were submitted to 264 students in 1969 who were actively involved in leadership and participant roles in black-student organizations on their campuses.[5] The schools were chosen at random and included the following regional breakdown: 3 in the South (32 respondents); 3 in the East (94 respondents); 8 in the Midwest (118 respondents); 1 in the West (19 respondents). Five were predominantly black or had very large (over 40 per cent) black-student enrollments. Two were two-year community colleges; 5 were four-year undergraduate schools, and the remainder had undergraduate and graduate programs. Eight were public (state or municipal); one was a Catholic university (21 respondents).

There was no significant difference in the number of male and female participants: 54 per cent male, 46 per cent female. This is significant, however, when one remembers that black female college enrollment throughout the country exceeds that of black males almost two to one! The average age was 21, with the women students averaging about six months younger than the men.

When asked to indicate their race, 64 per cent of the males listed "black"; 68 per cent of the women gave that designation. "Afro-American" was written by 16 per cent of the men and by 11 per cent of the women. "Negro" was used by 12 per cent of the men, and 20 per cent of the women. Out of the total of 264, not one student wrote "colored." Of those using the term "Negro," 53 per cent were from the South. There was a significant X^2 at the .05 level indicating that the region from which the student came had an effect on his use of the term "Negro." Students from the South tended to use the term "Negro" more than students from the other three regions.

[5] The data presented here are part of the author's research for a larger study, *They Demand Relevance: Black Students Protest*, to be published by Random House in 1970.

The students were asked if they believed it important to vote for either the Republican or Democratic presidential candidate. An overwhelming number (197) of the total respondents answered no, while only 57 answered yes. That is, 77.5 per cent did not believe this act of voting to be important; 22.5 per cent did believe so. Of the total of 57 answering yes, 54 (95 per cent) believed it more important to vote for the Democratic presidential candidate than for the Republican.

Some comparative data with white student activists are interesting in another category: career plans. Professor Richard Flacks's research of white students reveals the following:

> When asked to indicate their vocational aspirations, nonactivist students are typically firmly decided on a career and typically mention orientations toward the professions, science and business. Activists, on the other hand, are very frequently undecided on a career; and most typically those who have decided mention college teaching, the arts or social work as aspirations.[6]

When the black-student activists were asked if they were uncertain or fairly certain about their career plans, 76 per cent said they were fairly certain! Only 24 per cent were uncertain. While the questionnaire did not solicit specific vocations, innumerable discussions revealed that the fairly certain ones were oriented in the direction of Flacks's activist students, toward the service professions: teaching (elementary and secondary schools more so than college), social work, and a very heavy emphasis on "community organizing." Those who chose medicine or law almost always talked of starting community health clinics and community legal-aid services.

Religion has been a major part of the black American's life. While 85 per cent of the students grew up in families which professed a religion, 65 per cent indicated that they personally were not now adherents of a religion. Today's black-student activist is clearly rejecting the organized church of his parents. Most of them grew up in Baptist families (43 per cent), and, interestingly, the Catholic background outnumbered the Methodist—17 per cent to 11 per cent.

[6] Richard Flacks, "The Liberated Generation: An Exploration of the Roots of Student Protest," in Black Power and Student Rebellion, ed. James MeEvoy and Abraham Miller (Belmont, California, 1969), 371.

Of the 35 per cent who indicated a belief in a religion, 88 per cent of those adhered to the same religion as their parents.

The black students in the survey did not come from families nearly as financially well off as white-student activists, obviously. The data show 36 per cent reported family incomes below $5,000 per year; 44 per cent indicated family incomes between $5,000 and $8,999 per year. There were 14 per cent in the $9,000 to $13,999 category, and 6 per cent above $14,000.

Well over 50 per cent (152 respondents) were receiving some sort of scholarship aid in college, and only 80 students out of 264 reported that their fees, tuition, and expenses were paid in whole or in part by parents—not quite one third. Only 19 students (7 per cent) indicated they were supported solely by parents. The overwhelming majority were financing their education through a combination of sources: scholarships, working, parents, and loans. Of those who worked, 40 (15 per cent) indicated that employment was their sole means of support, while 113 (43 per cent) of the total were working to help finance their college education.

A survey of the educational background of the parents revealed the levels of formal education shown in Table 1. The information is based on information from the students of 497 parents.

TABLE 1

Education of Black Parents

Educational Level	Mother	Percentage	Father	Percentage	Total	Percentage
Eighth grade or less	28	11	47	19	75	15
More than eighth grade but not a high school graduate	67	26	59	24	126	25
High school graduate	90	35	76	31	166	33
Some college	45	18	25	10	70	14
College graduate	8	3	11	4	19	4
More than bachelor's degree	15	6	20	8	35	7
Unknown	2	1	4	4	6	2
Total	255	100	242	100	497	100

Black Studies

One of the major demands of black students has been the establishment of what has come to be called a "black studies" program. This demand has taken many forms: more courses dealing with black Americans; a distinct department with interdisciplinary courses (primarily social sciences and humanities) leading to a degree; a "school" or college within the larger university complex. All these proposals have in mind at least two things: first, a series of courses reflecting the "black experience"; and, second, a program geared to action. The students want the literature courses, for example, to reflect the writings and interpretations of black writers. They feel that this has been a noticeable gap in the offerings of modern literature. The black writers, it is felt, have a particular understanding of life in black America not shared by white writers, and this sensitivity is relevant to the lives of the black students. The same attitude exists with history courses dealing with Afro-Americans, and courses on the politics of black Americans. They want courses in these various fields which provide an understanding of the impact of the oral-communal nature of black culture on literature, politics, social structures, and so forth.

In addition, many students are demanding that these courses be made functional (relevant). That is, they want to be able to take the knowledge gained and go into the community and immediately begin to implement programs for social change. They are concerned about academia for action. They are distrustful of that higher academia that turns out scholars who do highly sophisticated research which ends up being discussed (and occasionally understood) only at selective professional meetings attended by a relatively small group of the researcher's colleagues. They want to be able to translate their knowledge into viable programs of action and change. And it is precisely at this point that the demands might conflict with the role of a university held by many in higher education, particularly in the social sciences.

Two major problems connected with these various proposals have centered around control and personnel. Many black students have insisted that the black studies programs will not be effective unless they are controlled by the black students and black faculty. They feel the white administrators and faculty have demonstrated their insensitivity to the kinds of changes being demanded, and thus will not permit the development of a relevant program. This speaks to the widening credibility gap between many black students and the universitites. Professor Vincent Harding has stated the problem in the following manner:

> Because they know their experiments are tender and fragile and in need of full protection in order to take root or be transformed, black students fight to protect both programs and people. This, too, is part of the meaning of the struggle for autonomous Black Studies programs. At a profound level, it is a part of the world-wide struggle of the formerly colonized peoples to find the freedom and initiative which will make it possible for them to experiment with and control those things which deeply affect their own lives and futures.
>
> ... The struggle for autonomy is also a sign of deep mistrust of the white universities. It is a profound challenge to the entire structure of the universities as we know them. Perhaps these institutions will not be able, in their present state of rigidity, to contain or adjust to the gropings of the students. But it is likely that black students will press on.[7]

Some black students have concluded that it is not possible to have a viable, autonomous black studies department at a predominantly white university, thus they have called for the establishment of black-controlled institutions. The black students at Merritt College in Oakland, California issued such a call, as did a group that recently formed The Malcolm X Liberation University in Durham, North Carolina.

Many universities and colleges are willing to establish black studies programs, but they insist that standards for hiring personnel be consistent with standards for other departments. Thus, the professor with a Ph.D. is highly sought. But many black students no longer believe in the efficacy of those traditional standards. At times they demand that people be hired who, for a number of reasons, do not have the traditional credentials of higher academia. Those credentials, it is felt, have not been a particularly meaningful barometer for relevance in the past, and there is no reason to suspect otherwise now.

What sort of standards should be adopted in evaluating the student's work? Should special consideration be given black students? Would this not result in a dual grading system, which could have serious negative repercussions for the morale of the whole campus? Should the students, with clearly discernible handicaps (in verbal

[7] Vincent Harding, "Black Students and the 'Impossible Revolution,'" *Ebony*, August 1969, 145.

and mathematical skills, for example) be admitted without a well-thought-out, fully developed remedial program? Should emphasis be placed on recruiting students for the two-year community-college programs, which might prepare them better for university work later? If this is done, how does one avoid the possibility that such programs might become no more than vocational training grounds and terminal points in the student's formal education? Obviously, there are many different answers, depending on the kind of university, its location, and its resources. But there are some general statements that can be made about these problems.

One of the most detrimental developments in this entire field would be the attempt to put together black studies departments which promise more on paper than they can deliver in fact. It is one thing for a university to offer a few new courses on black literature, the politics of the black community, and the history of black Americans where there are materials and talent to warrant such courses. This should be done. But it is entirely another, and an undesirable, thing to list courses with elaborate descriptions if there is not a legitimate body of literature and thought to justify them.

The most fruitful thing the major universities could do at this time is to establish legitimate research programs to support the protracted, empirical research necessary to inform a new body of black studies literature. Clearly, there is much work to be done. Old hypotheses and assumptions need to be questioned in the light of recent, real developments in the society; new questions must be asked and answered. For example, much of the literature in political science overlooks the importance of the black church (and minister) as an agent of politicization. Virtually nothing is known about the relationship between the American political process and political traumatization (as opposed to political apathy) in the black community. One needs to know much more about the impact of the oral tradition of the black culture on the politics of spokesmanship in the black community. What are the implications for subsequent public policy and the development of viable community, social, and political structures for change? As new, hard data are obtained in such areas of inquiry, it will be possible to talk meaningfully about the black experience. These are the kinds of questions that would justify a distinct discipline known as black studies, a discipline that would cut across traditional disciplinary boundaries. When answered, these kinds of questions could lay to rest the polemical, premature pronouncements like the following: "To recruit thousands of young blacks into hitherto restricted American universities and to fill their heads full of something called black studies is to prepare them for nothing. The favorable response by universities to the demand for such curricula should make blacks suspicious."[8] Such statements characterize the level of much of the discussion of black studies and do not in any way speak to the serious and potentially useful contribution that a carefully organized black studies program could make to increased knowledge and effect social change.

Most colleges and universities are probably not prepared, financially or otherwise, to launch extensive research programs. In such cases, those places of higher education should not attempt to establish elaborate, but superficial, black studies departments. The intensive political atmosphere created by the demands makes a hasty response understandable, but inexcusable.

The argument made here is not against black studies, but for a program where the talent and resources justify one. It is possible now to move rapidly in some places toward a major in the areas of the arts, the humanities, and possibly history, but that is probably the limit at this time.

Much of the public discussion thus far of black studies has centered on dramatic, glamorous issues such as who would control the programs (the question of autonomy), whether the programs would be used as platforms for ideological proselyting, and whether white professors and white students would be permitted to participate. The important issue of substance has usually been overlooked. The fact is that if a black studies program is not substantively sound, it does not matter who controls it or what it is used for or who participates in it. And if the quality of the program measures up to rigorous academic standards—standards which require that hypotheses be stated and tested by careful accumulation of data—the problems of control, content, and participation will not be insurmountable.

Recruitment and Admissions

In virtually all instances where black students are protesting in predominantly white colleges, the demand is to recruit and admit more black students. As is generally known, the overall enrollment of

[8] Arnold Beichman, "As the Campus Civil War Goes On, Will Teacher Be the New Drop-Out?" The New York Times Magazine, December 7, 1969, 48.

black students in Northern white colleges has been exceptionally low over the years. Likewise, one (certainly not the only) reason has been the inability of universities to find sufficiently large numbers of black students who could qualify by traditional measurements in the highly competitive arena of college admissions.

Many demands are for preferential treatment for black students, both in terms of spaces allotted and criteria used to judge qualification. Some schools have moved in this direction by relying less on college-board scores and more on "intangible" criteria such as motivation and perceived potential for success.

Several schools have supported recruitment efforts by their own black students who would go to high schools to talk to potential applicants in an effort to increase enrollment. The thinking in these instances has been that the black-student recruiters could establish a better relationship with the high school student than an adult recruiter and give the student a more accurate picture of university life, academic and social. It is entirely too soon to assess the effectiveness of these efforts.

The problem of admitting more black students to colleges was highlighted by events at Rutgers University and at the City University of New York in 1969. Demands were made for "open enrollment." Rutgers agreed to admit all minority students from Newark, New Brunswick, and Camden. Fears were expressed in many circles that such policies would lower academic standards, and several universities understood that extensive remedial programs would have to be devised if the new students were to survive beyond the first year.

In the final analysis, one must come to recognize that the problem of preparing a student for entry into and survival in the college environment must begin long before the student has finished high school. A fruitful long-term approach would be to have the universities (initially through their departments and schools of education) become intimately involved in the elementary and secondary education process in the schools in the black community. Waiting until the student is at the point of applying to college is passing on the major burden of catching up to the colleges. The universities should have elaborate cooperative programs (much more than the traditional practice-teaching) with the community schools from the first through the twelfth grades. Such a relationship should permit a wide range of experimental programs with the university working closely with the local school board, the various school administrators, teachers, students, and parents. This would involve new techniques of teaching, new instructional materials, and developing new concepts of school-community relations. It is easy to see how black college students could involve themselves in such a program. The main point is that the university, especially the university in close proximity to impacted urban areas, could become an integral, substantive part of the educational process in the community at the elementary and secondary levels. Government, foundations, and private industry should be turned to as sources of funds and expertise in implementing such programs. "College" should begin in elementary school in a serious way. Only then would it make sense to talk about the possibility of substantially increased enrollments at the university level later.

Finally, many of the problems such as control of black studies programs and admissions based on competition or preferential treatment are results of the immediate *political* environment in which the demands are being raised. The universities, like many other institutions, are caught in the middle of dynamic social forces contending for power and change. How these forces are dealt with depends on a complex of specific, indigenous factors which lend themselves to delicate political considerations as well as to academic concerns. One must, in other words, understand the current demands in their political context.

The emphasis of this article does not intend to minimize the difficulty of current political problems. Rather it chooses to focus on the long-term, substantive, academic concerns for two main reasons. First, each school must work out its own local political problems under circumstances peculiar to each campus. Second, it is only by beginning to deal with the long-term, substantive issues can there be any hope for eventually alleviating the serious problems which give rise to recurring political demands. Tackling the substantive issues is a tedious, nonglamorous task. It does not capture headlines and provide dramatic confrontations. But, in these times of emotionalism and heated ferment, the university must assume the responsibility of charting a direction which rises above the immediate concerns and looks to the future. It does not seem unreasonable to ask the universities to assume this role. It is a role which puts the university in the forefront of social change and development in crucial activities—research and educational involvement. No other institution in the society should be expected to be in the vanguard in the performance of those functions.

The Community and the Campus

FRANKLIN H. WILLIAMS

The corporation, in this society, at this time in history, is not something separate from the surrounding community. In its self-interest, therefore, the corporation must make an effort to help improve the quality of life in the society of which it is an integral part. Hard-headed businessmen have begun to realize that, and while the "business of business is business," the public weal must also be its business.

Universities, too, are becoming aware that their well-being is dependent on the health of society. Consequently, there are now more than seventy-five urban institutes and urban centers across the country working hard to deliver their skills and knowledge to the solution of problems in their surrounding communities.

By 1985 the 12 million blacks now in the central cities will have grown to 20 million. The nation's largest cities will have black majorities by then—Washington, D.C., and Newark already do. In addition, the population of other minority groups is growing in many cities —Puerto Ricans in New York and Mexican-Americans in Los Angeles and Denver, for example. This phenomenal growth of minority-group populations—about 150 per cent of the increase of the white majority—will heighten the pressures on urban-based institutions for services and support and compound the problem of delivering such services. Already the pressure is being felt in education, housing, and health care; and the needs in these and other areas will increase substantially.

Business is already making efforts to respond positively to the urban crisis through such efforts as the Urban Coalition, the National

Alliance of Businessmen, and the efforts of individual companies. One of these groups is the New Detroit Committee, formed in that city after the 1967 riot, to plan for the rebuilding of the city. The committee, composed of Detroit's most prominent businessmen as well as some of its most-outspoken black militants, pushed for an open-housing law, reform of tenant-landlord law, and housing-code enforcement in the state legislature. As a result of the committee's efforts, General Motors and Ford hired additional black workers; the J. L. Hudson Company, Detroit's largest department store, hired and trained 500 of the hard-core unemployed; and the Michigan Bell Telephone Company lent training personnel and facilities to a high school near the riot zone.

In New York the late Senator Robert Kennedy was the prime mover behind two corporations which sought the help of business and industry to create new opportunities for the residents of Brooklyn's Bedford-Stuyvesant ghetto. One of them, the Restoration Corporation, is run by community residents, who determine what development, rehabilitation, and service projects will be undertaken; and the other, the Development and Services Corporation, enlists the cooperation and advice of some of New York's top corporation executives in the Bedford-Stuyvesant effort.

In Philadelphia, in 1968, the major businesses gave $1 million to a group called the Black Coalition, representing a broad range of black groups, to use as they saw fit. In addition, the city's four savings banks started a $20-million pool to make below-market interest-rate mortgage money available to low-income families for buying homes in six of the city's rundown neighborhoods.

In spite of these and other programs, there is still a gap of major proportions which corporations must help to close. While black and other minority communities are less than 15 per cent of the population, they constitute a substantially greater percentage of the unemployed. In this statistic there are interesting implications for both the corporate and the educational communities.

In the first place a thoughtless comparison is often made. It is said that the new immigrants to the cities should be able to "make it" as the earlier European immigrants did at the turn of the century. Conditions are significantly different than they were then, however, and work to the disadvantage of those at the bottom of the urban ladder. In the late nineteenth and early twentieth centuries the American economy was expanding rapidly, and there were many jobs for unskilled workers. There were subway tunnels to dig, railroads to lay, and offices and apartments to build. Now there are fewer opportunities for this kind of work, and most of the existing jobs are controlled by unions whose leadership is still in the hands of the descendants of those earlier immigrants. Blacks and other minorities cannot easily crack the barriers to employment which are placed in their way.

In addition, it is not easy to be poor and patient today. During the earlier immigration waves, the migrants were isolated in their ghettos, speaking their own languages, but today the mass media constantly taunt the ghetto with the affluence of modern society.

Today, the jobs which will provide the "leg up" that earlier immigrants got from unskilled labor require education and training. For example, 97 per cent of the total increase in employment between 1947 and 1963 was in white-collar jobs. These are jobs which require at least a high school education and often some specialized training as well. Compare this figure with another one. Only 4.6 per cent of the college students in America today are black, and most of these are in black colleges in the South. The implications of these two sets of statistics are clear. Blacks are not being prepared for the existing job market.

Higher educational institutions in the last few years have been in a race to enroll black students—but only "qualified" black students. The catch here, of course, is that ghetto life and schools are not likely to turn out vast quantities of "qualified" students in the traditional sense of the term. Hard-core city minorities, hampered by poverty, discrimination, family instability, and poor elementary education, find themselves trapped in a constantly continuing circle of deprivation, denial, and bitterness.

What is called for in the long run is a complete overhaul of the public school system to make it responsive to the needs of inner-city residents; but, in the meantime, today's high school students need higher education. The answer is not "lower" standards for college admission but "different" standards—standards which recognize the skills, strong points, and motivation of the ghetto student, who may not be able to say that "zenith" is the opposite of "nadir" on a college board examination but who has had complete responsibility for the care of younger brothers and sisters since he was ten years old.

The responsibility for the education of this group of American citizens cannot be left entirely to public institutions. Private colleges and universities have to do their part as well, or the circle of denial will never be broken. Many universities are beginning to recognize this and are recruiting socially and economically deprived students on the basis of motivation rather than simply academic achievement.

But this effort faces serious hurdles and creates special problems, for there is a pitiful shortage of resources and the need increases in direct proportion to the degree that institutions undertake this effort. Ghetto students must have more scholarship aid, more supportive services and even subsidies, probably double what the average white student needs. Many times such students come from families where their loss as a wage earner really hurts.

Louis Nieves, executive director of Aspira, a Puerto Rican agency concerned with higher education and community leadership, recently pointed out this problem in an interview with the New York *Times*. He charged that 65 per cent of a group of Puerto Rican students who had been attending colleges in the New York area had dropped out before graduating. He felt that this high dropout rate—20 per cent higher than the national norm of 40 to 45 per cent—could be attributed to the failure of colleges to "understand the education of minority groups." Colleges, he thinks, need to give more attention to financial aid, a special curriculum to make up for previous deficiencies, and bilingual teaching for Spanish-speaking students.

Lewis Mayhew, former president of the American Association for Higher Education, also recognizing the problem, has said that the major universities must be willing to support black graduate students for a year or two years of pregraduate work. "The states must be prepared to offer massive scholarships of from $2,000 to $3,000 a year for black youth regardless of past academic achievement and regardless of whether or not the students appreciate it." He went on to recommend that American higher education expand its capacity to handle from 70,000 to a million additional students, the number required to make enrollment proportional. If private universities are to contribute to the needed expansion, they will need more facilities, more faculty, and more financial aid.

And how can the corporation help? What can business do to ease this crisis? Increased contributions to colleges and universities! It just makes good business sense. The universities are the main source of corporate recruitment now—and they are smart to protect that source for the future. But the corporation's interest in the university and the urban crisis should go even further.

The corporation must work with the university—for example, the Esso Education Foundation's lively new magazine, *Change,* which is exploring new directions in higher education, trying to find some sensible solutions to problems of urban education. Another natural link between corporations and universities is in the area of educational technology. Great strides are being made by the electronics and communications industries in developing teaching machines, computers, and other devices for use in classrooms. Little has been done, however, to adapt the new technology specifically to the needs of ghetto schools and the pedagogy of educationally deprived students. This would seem to be a logical place for corporations and educational institutions to pool their expertise and develop new educational programs for minority-group students.

The corporation must also cooperate with university-community projects. In the area of small business there is a great deal that can be done. Actually, there was more black business in the past than there is today. At one time there were sixty-eight black-owned banks compared to today's twenty-one—and, according to a recent article in *The Nation,* even the number of black-owned businesses in Harlem has dropped by one-third.

Candidates for the master of business administration degree in the Graduate School of Business at Columbia University have organized the M.B.A. Management Consultants, Inc., to offer small-business men in Harlem technical assistance. The school also works with the university's purchasing department in an effort to direct more of Columbia's purchases toward the Harlem community. To implement this the university recently opened a purchasing office in Harlem, assigning a black staff member to work there.

It would make good sense for corporations to encourage the development of businesses in ghetto areas such as Harlem. In the first place, black-owned businesses would provide outlets for products not presently being marketed in these areas. In addition, through expanded programs of loans and technical assistance, businesses owned by minority-group members could be started which would feed into existing larger businesses. For example, a company manufacturing television sets, which contracts the assembling of some of the component parts to other companies, could help a minority-group businessman get started and provide him with initial contracts, while he in turn could employ workers, who would then be earning enough money to buy new television sets.

In housing and economic development, Columbia's School of Architecture is using the university's facilities and resources to interest business leaders in the problems of the city. Their action projects include a jitney bus system for Harlem, a community institute for real estate management, a housing consortium which, incidentally, involves the Celanese Corporation and American Standard.

In the School of General Studies, a new Development Division is offering courses in basic math, community organization, and computer training to community groups. This is a nondegree program and, as such, is not subject to the usual qualifying conditions and standards of admission. It provides greater flexibility in designing courses which fit the immediate needs of students.

Another project, something quite new, is the awarding of fellowships to minority-group students in premedical education. This is expensive and involves a high-risk area because many who begin may fall by the wayside. The need for more minority-group doctors is urgent, however, and additional seed money is required for programs of this sort.

This issue leads to another facet of university-community relations and the corporation. In medical schools today there are only a few more black students enrolled than there were twenty years ago. In those days, black students pursued medicine, dentistry, law, teaching, and religion. These were the only avenues to success open to them and they could practice their professions only in the black community. Now there are wider opportunities for black professionals, and private industry is also competing for black college graduates. To the degree that the search succeeds, the result is to siphon off those who previously would have been trained in the professions to serve black people. It is tempting to accept a job paying $20,000 a year as a corporation executive rather than face the prospect of establishing a dental practice in a poor black neighborhood.

This brain drain will contribute to the deterioration of services in the inner city unless professional schools can offer increased financial help to attract and support minority-group men and women who will return to their communities as young doctors, dentists, and lawyers. The corporate community must realize that universities which have been their staff training and recruitment service are now attempting to serve urban needs as well. It is imperative that corporations help universities train increasing numbers of students from these depressed and suffering city centers. To do this is fantastically expensive.

A word of caution is in order here. The universities and the corporations have not been known in the past for their sensitivity to the needs of minority communities, nor have they been quick to move toward changing their traditional roles. Urban universities are beginning to see that they have a responsibility to serve the communities that surround them, but it will take a long time to break down the barriers of suspicion and mistrust between the university and the ghetto.

By the same token, corporations cannot expect that their contributions will be received with unanimous expressions of gratitude. Quite the contrary. It is more likely that corporate gifts and loans will initially be looked on by students and minority-group communities as an attempt to "buy them off." Corporations will have to prove their good will.

Nor can corporations expect to control the resources which they place in universities and black communities. In this day when the slogan "community control" is applied to every ghetto institution from schools to hospitals, corporations must be willing to serve as advisers, not manipulators; and, while providing resources for educational and economic development, they must allow ghetto residents to shape their own future.

Traditionally, the university and the corporation have been linked for the mutual benefit of each. Now this historic relationship must serve new ends. The university today must change its direction and stand as a new Statue of Liberty for the American people—beckoning to its doors the deprived and depressed masses trapped in the urban areas. But it cannot let them in, nurture their minds and spirits, and prepare them to overcome society's ills without financial help—on a massive scale.

The New Concept of "Community"

JAMES M. HESTER

The term "community" has several different meanings to colleges and universities. It can mean the community from which a university draws students—a national or a local community. It can be the community of employers who are served by students trained at the university, and thus again it can be a national or a local community. And for some institutions, the community can consist of a group of residents who receive a variety of direct services from the educational institution in the form of adult education and, increasingly, community service projects sometimes sponsored by businesses and carried out by faculty and students.

The fact should be recognized that by and large the corporations have related themselves to these concepts of the campus for reasons of self-interest—employee relations or public relations. In stating it this way, no criticism is implied. The ultimate guide for any function of business has been its profitability.

Such programs as tuition for employees and their children, national scholarship programs, matching-gift programs, and grants for special projects within the universities have certainly been related primarily to self-interest—to employee relations or to public relations. Some programs have been more broadly based, such as the support for graduate education as a contribution to the national need for more Ph.D. graduates, and certainly the rich support that many universities have received in capital campaigns has taken into account the general needs of society. Universities are supported in their fund campaigns by corporations simply on the basis that a better university is good for the nation and for the businesses that function within it. In recent years both universities and corporations have come to recognize the importance of responding to the full needs of society.

The first of these needs has to do with the disadvantaged. Many corporations have taken a new look at their training practices in order to accommodate a greater number of people whose previous training did not qualify them immediately for jobs in industry. Colleges and universities have collaborated with the corporations by providing training programs for persons whose previous experience would not have qualified them for normal entry into business.

Many colleges have instituted work-study programs for students from disadvantaged backgrounds, combining a relationship with specific businesses that provide tuition, summer jobs, and part-time jobs during the school year. Here again a partnership has been worked out between the corporations and the universities not based solely on the immediate interest of the corporation but on a recognition of a serious social need. Bonds have already been formed in relation to other so-called urban problems such as air pollution, water pollution, traffic problems, noise problems, and the health services in urban areas. Many research grants, however, that universities have received for studies of air pollution can be directly related to the industry involved either in its attempt to meet new regulations in the control of its own polluting effects or because it wished to find new methods of selling a product that help solve the problems of air pollution. As a result of the reevaluation of society that has been imposed by the conditions and realizations of the sixties, the universities have accepted new concepts of their community, and a new focus of the obligation they have to society and to its disadvantaged members by providing new kinds of educational opportunities for both the local and the national community. In part this is a response to the social conscience of the academic community composed of the faculty and the students. They demand that educational institutions play a more vigorous role in providing opportunities for the disadvantaged to use the colleges and universities as means for entering the mainstream of American life.

It is not sufficient simply to expand public educational institutions to accommodate disadvantaged groups. If the nation is going to provide vigorous and inviting channels for the brightest members of minority groups to enter the professions, to work for corporations, and to run for public office, then opportunities must be provided in the most highly qualified institutions for those who are able to meet their educational standards. When financial assistance has been available, many qualified members of disadvantaged groups were unexpectedly found. That is one of the great lessons of the past five years.

There is no adequate source of financial support to universities for the kind of commitment that is needed. And most universities have overextended themselves in attempting to meet the needs. Half of the current deficit of New York University, for example, is the result of overcommitments to scholarships and special counseling for black students. The federal government has provided some assistance, but that has been limited. The state governments have provided some, but that has been insufficient. Corporations have responded to the needs in a variety of ways. Many have established their own training programs, others have joined combinations of corporations in training programs, and others have supported the Urban Coalition. The amount of money that is received from corporations either as a total amount for higher education or for individual universities cannot possibly meet the costs if they are to do the job of providing a new kind of educational opportunity, particularly for the black community.

It is highly important that corporations, therefore, reevaluate their social investment in higher education based, as many corporate leaders have suggested, on a concern for the viability of the society in which they must operate and on the valuation of business and industry by the society. Both educational institutions and corporations are being scrutinized by students with a perspective that is far more intense and more challenging than any experienced before. They are demanding that the universities and corporations measure up to standards of social service that are more extensive, more embracing, than those the campus or the corporation has been willing to accept in the past. Since these young men and women will determine the future success of all institutions of the society, it is necessary to rethink the principles and the standards by which one judges what is adequate in the support of social values. This thinking cannot be related solely to current profit and loss, to public relations, or to employee relations. It can only be related to a long-term evaluation of where society is going and the role that industry will play in its development.

University Research

J. R. KILLIAN, JR.

The university has become one of the primary institutions of American society. It has the responsibility for most of the nation's basic research and scholarly studies. It provides education for both undergraduate and graduate students and for the professional talent our complex society requires. In addition, it is called upon to perform a great array of public services where expertise is required and to provide consultants or advisers to government and to business and industry. As Clark Kerr has said, "Knowledge is now central to society. It is wanted, even demanded, by more people and more institutions than ever before."

The United States is indeed becoming a research-dependent society. In almost every aspect of life, the nation relies more and more on knowledge-seeking, problem-solving techniques. Almost every activity, not just technology, is invigorated by research—law, management, economics and the other social sciences, the political process, and even the arts. And in these times of stress and crises, the scholar in his study and the scientist and engineer in their laboratories are looked to for ideas and problem solving to cope with a deteriorating environment, with pollution, poverty, and the arms race.

Let me examine the role of American universities in scientific and engineering research. During the past several decades, university science in the United States has yielded a spectacular harvest, and American science has achieved unquestioned world leadership. For ready indices of this accomplishment, recall some of the now almost trite statistics. From 1900 to 1930, American scientists received only seven out of ninety-three Nobel Prizes. In the 1950s, they received thirty out of fifty-four. And in the 1960s, Americans received twenty-eight out of fifty-seven. As I. I. Rabi once pointed out, the *American Physical Review* in 1927 did not command much attention by European physicists; but by 1937, it had become the leading journal of physics in the world. Today, in the literature of world science, reference to American scientific journals exceeds those of all other foreign scientific publications. And, parenthetically, some statistician with time on his hands figured out that about 15 per cent of all the words ever written on scientific subjects were written in 1967!

The place which American science had achieved, especially in the universities, prior to World War II, was profoundly important to the winning of the war. The vigor of the American economy has resulted in part from the new industries, new processes, and new products generated in the scientific laboratories of the nation. While American science was achieving world leadership, so was the nation's industrial strength.

In this great intellectual surge, American colleges and universities have been major contributors. Of all the Nobel Prizes won by scientists in the United States, something like eighty-five out of ninety have been received by university scientists. Clearly, the university has become the principal home of basic research in the United States, and the quality of the research has been superb. This does not mean that important basic research has not been carried out by other types of institutions. Indeed, it has flourished in a few distinguished industrial and governmental laboratories, and in private research institutes. But the major responsibility for basic research has rested with the universities, with the industrial laboratories drawing sustenance from this basic research and themselves specializing brilliantly in applied research.

It is the special strength of university research that it is imbedded in the process of education. Science education must take place in the provocative, generative environment of creativity, with the young apprentice scientist himself learning by research, and in this way gaining the insights, the skills, and the outlook which are in combination essential for productive scientists.

Another important achievement in the domain of science and engineering in the United States has been the interaction between the scientific communities in the universities and those in industry and government. This close relationship has made it possible for new ideas, new discoveries, and new data to flow more easily from university laboratory to application, and it has especially accelerated the process of bringing the results of basic research rapidly into effective use.

This process of putting science to work has also been aided by the close interrelationship in many university laboratories between basic research and applied research, between science and engineering. This partnership serves to stimulate and enrich both science and technology. Universities are uniquely able to facilitate interdisciplinary communication, and this affords them special opportunities to achieve innovation.

The great university centers of teaching and research in science and engineering have been one of the principal sources of industrial advance. The spectacularly successful role of the Land Grant colleges in the United States in fostering high-yield agriculture has long been recognized. It has been basic research systematically made available to farmers that has made possible the spectacular increase in yields of corn and wheat. As a result of their research, universities have likewise played a major role in the generation of new industry. Research and development in scientific and engineering institutions made major contributions to the origin and growth of the computer industry. The chemical, electrical, and nuclear industries have derived much from research carried out in both university and nonuniversity laboratories.

Research in the universities has provided a steady succession of medical discoveries vital to the health of the nation, and technology generated in universities has contributed to the spectacular success of the space program, including the safe landing of men on the moon and their return. Inertial guidance and navigation for missiles and space vehicles is the product of a world-famous laboratory in one of our institutes of technology. Engineering research in institutes of technology has provided fundamental concepts underlying the development of catalytic cracking in the oil industry; and the development of digitally controlled machine tools, one of the most important industrial advances of our time, took place in the laboratory of an institute of technology.

Today America is witnessing the opening up of new domains of science which can have profound effects upon society. This is a period of major biological discoveries which are yielding great advances in medicine and are unravelling the mysteries of genetics (and, as a result, are raising profound ethical and social questions). There is a growing collaboration in universities between the life sciences and engineering, particularly between medicine and engineering. Applied scientists and engineers in the universities are turning their attention to such socially important fields as energy conversion, transportation, and environmental control. Many of the environmental and ecological problems that now require urgent attention must in part be solved by bringing to bear in new ways the resources of science and engineering. This can only be done, however, through effective community and political leadership and through the adaptation of political organizations to deal with pollution and similar problems in new ways.

The future record of the universities in basic research and in the education of creative scientists and engineers will result in part from the stimulus of young minds working closely with older minds. Research in the pure sciences certainly seems to flourish best when there is an interplay between students and teachers, each invigorating the other. Students who have studied the conditions conducive to effective research have also pointed out that creative work tends to flourish best in an environment that is adaptive rather than authoritarian. The open environment of the university, with its freedom of inquiry, its emphasis on the individual, and its lack of a hierarchical organization, seems to be important in the conduct of successful research. The university environment is also benign because it provides interaction between many different disciplines. Perhaps one of the most important factors in the American economy of today and in the present state of industrial activity has been the opportunity in universities for science, engineering, management, and the social sciences to work together side by side, each having an impact upon the other.

Today universities, particularly their programs in science and engineering, are moving into a critical period. The government is cutting back on funds for research, and in a manner that is unplanned and therefore the more damaging. This cutback is made much more serious by steady inflation. The drastic cutbacks in government support are not only curtailing the amount of research, the quality of the research, and the training of men and women to do research, but it threatens the breakup of experienced teams and the closing of major facilities. It threatens to erode the preeminent position of the United States in science and technology.

The nation also is undergoing a period of skepticism about the benign uses of science and technology, and there is too much of a tendency to blame science and technology for their misuse rather than dealing with the more central problem of how to direct these great resources toward more humane ends. The way to ensure a humane environment and advance the quality of society is not by cutting back on science and engineering advances, particularly at a stage of flood tide in creativity in these fields, but rather in mastering the problems of control and use, of technology assessment, and of foresight. The universities have a major role to play in helping to put science and research to use for humane purposes.

The present adverse view of science has been summarized by one of our distinguished physicists, Professor Victor F. Weisskopf:

> Today science is attacked from two opposite fronts: One is a mounting public opinion shared by some members of Congress and Government, that the study of nature for its own sake, the search for deeper explanations of natural phenomena is an expensive luxury, which should be supported only if it promises immediate pay-off in terms of practical applications for industry or medicine.
>
> The other attack comes from opinions held by a significant part of the younger generation: Science is distrusted as being the source of industrial innovations leading to further deterioration of our environment, to further destructive applications in weaponry, and to further developments in our society toward a world of Orwell's 1984. At best, they say, pure science is a waste of resources which would be better devoted to some immediate socially useful purposes.
>
> Both attacks are based upon a misinterpretation of the nature of science. Science is the cornerstone of our modern civilization in many respects. The effort to understand our natural environment is man's most successful collective enterprise in history. It has created new ways of thinking and new ways of life. It has thoroughly reshaped our mental and physical environment. The difficulties of our day are caused by the growing rate of technological change and by the growing expansion of technology. They do not stem from the failure of science, but from its unexpected strength. The numerous problems, which the rapidly expanding application of science has created, can be solved only by painstaking investigations of the effects of industrialization and by a thorough study of the interrelation of many factors which determine our environment. To do so needs more basic science and not less of it.

The careful analysis of the problems and the necessary measures of solving them will require more, not less, of the spirit engendered in pure research. We will need more, not fewer, people trained in the unbiased search of causes and effects. The scientists who are involved in fundamental research have always proved to be the best reservoir of manpower for tasks which require objectivity, innovative ideas and imaginative approaches. We must not let the source of this reservoir dry up.[1]

In this period of financial crisis in the universities, it is of the greatest importance to understand the dangers to the nation in permitting the great resources that have been built to erode or be dispersed. There has never been a time when the private sources of support for universities and for research have had a greater role to play in maintaining the continuing vigor and contribution of these scholarly activities. Let us not now lose our nerve. We have hardly begun the great intellectual adventure of understanding nature and of controlling environment.

[1] Victor F. Weisskopf in a privately circulated statement.

The Use of University Resources

W. CLARKE WESCOE

The university occupies a unique position in the affairs of men. It is considered with affection by most, if not all, of its alumni; it is regarded by parents with admiration as the institution which will provide their children with a foundation for productive and meaningful living; it is nurtured by government, in underdeveloped as well as developed nations, with the knowledge that strength and growth depend upon a broadly educated citizenry; it is sustained, in part, by the corporate community, for the ideas generated within it and the young people who depart from it represent much of the future of that community. And yet, withal, it is looked upon as a disturbing element, at some time by almost all with a sense of suspicion. All this is true because, if it is to fulfill its vital function, a university must produce an unsettling influence.

The university was designed to be a change-making institution. It produces changes in people, in technology, in human relations, and in human affairs. The university functions to conserve and to transmit knowledge, to enlarge upon and extend it, to expand horizons and to open up a brighter future. It was created by man to provide a key to unlock the future. To fulfill that purpose it is necessary to challenge the status quo; that challenge is the source of the uneasiness created by the university in the minds of many.

In general, humankind, like all other species, feels most comfortable in unchanging surroundings. There is a comfort to be derived from predictability, to know that tomorrow will be much like today. It is the unknown that produces fear and discomfort; in medical affairs it is called dis-ease. Universities are meant to explore the unknown. They are meant to examine all ideas, no matter how repugnant those ideas may be to some. The true university rejects nothing out of hand. It is committed to the search for greater, more enduring truths in the recognition that ultimate truth continues to elude us. It is to the lasting credit of man that he created such an institution. It is not surprising, however, that occasionally he views it with suspicion, if not outright distrust.

The university has been looked upon as a citadel of theory, not always practical, often slow-moving. The "theorists" within it have been looked upon as being incapable of practice. In the most pejorative sense they have been described by the detractors in a time-worn cliché as being those who could not "do" and therefore taught. Nothing, of course, could be further from the truth. The theories expounded on university campuses have found their way successfully to the market place. The consultative services of the theorists have been sought avidly by government and by industry, sometimes to the point where the theorists became well-traveled and spent more time off-campus than on.

As individuals have in the past, universities as entities are now beginning to address themselves to practical participation in human affairs. The enormous strengths available in their various faculties are being catalyzed into coordinated efforts to attack difficult problems off the campus. These efforts have been slow in coming, have been started gingerly, and rightly so, for too great an involvement as an institution in current affairs can threaten the very existence of the institution. The world continues to need islands of contemplation, the source of new theories, the possessor of moral and not practical force. Universities are not geared for the continual prosecution or administration of large-scale projects in the community. That is what government, corporations, and other entities are best able to do. The great strength of the future rests in a close relationship between the university and these other agencies so that proven theory can be put into meaningful practice.

Efficiency of University Operations

Universities have been criticized for inefficiency and lack of economy in their operations. Perhaps the most common belief is that the principle of tenure to which universities are committed leads to inefficient performance on the part of the faculty and perpetuates mediocrity in its membership. But the principle of tenure is a foundation stone of academic performance. It is not granted lightly, nor should it be. It is an essential to an institution committed to the continual search for truth and the examination of ideas, no matter how unnecessary such examination may appear to some. It protects the individual who has committed himself to such an institution from reprisal, politically or emotionally motivated. To be sure, an occasional mistake may be made by an institution, an occasional member may fail to fulfill his predicted potential and become unproductive. That occasional error, which can be proved only retrospectively, is a small price to pay for a principle so important. Other human organizations make such mistakes; the corporation is not immune to them.

In a similar fashion universities have been criticized relative to the number of teaching hours assigned to faculty members. The ultimate extension of this criticism is that faculty members are paid very well but work very little. Universities have not attempted adequately to explain their procedures in this area. Nine classroom hours per week seem like a small enough effort to the uninformed. Forgotten are the hours of preparation required to make each classroom hour most productive; overlooked are the hours of consultation with graduate students and other students outside the classroom. The provision of time for the faculty to carry out the research necessary for the extension of knowledge is a requirement of the university just as is the allocation of time for work on vital university functions which demand the time of faculty for committee work. The usual faculty member works long hours, generally longer hours than almost any professional. There are few windows dark in the evening hours on a university campus; the laboratories and libraries are in active use while most townspeople are enjoying their rest.

There is also a common belief that universities are inefficient because too many courses are provided for student selection. This belief is held by those who would neatly compartmentalize human knowledge and, perhaps, ignore those areas whose courses lead to cultural understanding and advancement. A university to be worthy of its name must provide balanced offerings; these offerings need not be kaleidoscopic, but they must be broad enough to ensure quality undergraduate and graduate education. Additionally, concern with other areas of the world dictate the institution of new programs which twenty years ago may have appeared purely esoteric.

There are those, as well, accustomed to seeing public schools closed from late afternoon to morning and desolate in the summer months, who believe that universities utilize their investment in physical facilities poorly or profligately. What those poorly informed or unobservant do not appreciate is that universities operate on a full-day, round-the-clock, year-round basis. The evening hours are just as full as the daylight ones. The summer months are filled with general course offerings and programs for executives, professionals, and others that cannot be carried on in other months of the year.

Strangely, too, there are frequently voiced beliefs that universities are becoming too big, as if to indicate that bigness is of itself a detriment to an institution. That is strange in a nation where bigness in other enterprises is looked upon as a sign of success. There are economies inherent in larger size; there is a critical mass beyond which more can be done at less cost. Size in itself is no criterion of quality in an educational program. There are some first-class schools of limited size, and there are some very poor ones; similarly there are leading institutions of substantial size, and some of substantial size that are less than good. Quality depends not upon size but upon a multitude of factors, abstract and concrete.

Finally, there is a widespread belief that universities are centers of liberalism or radicalism, that university faculty members lean to the left of center in their teaching. There is no way in which an institution committed to the examination of all ideas, tolerant to the opinions of many, can dispel that belief. Careful scrutiny will reveal, however, that faculties and institutions share with others a certain resistance to change and a middle-of-the-road approach to most problems.

University Management

Because the university is a unique institution there are inherent limitations in its management. These limitations have produced frustrations alike in those who are charged with its administration and those who look upon it from the outside, sometimes in bewilderment. Some of its aspects are purely financial in nature and lend themselves to ease of analysis; most of its aspects are involved with scholarship and creativity, and literally defy analysis.

The necessity of providing an atmosphere conducive to creative work and scholarship makes university management difficult. There are no useful parameters of measurement available to gauge payout on investments or continuing operational expenditures. The efficiency of a creative enterprise in which tangible results are difficult to assess practically defies evaluation. Decisions must be made on the basis of how best scholarship may be advanced.

Decisions in a university are, perhaps, more the result of consensus than in any other enterprise. The university president cannot be autocratic; he must rely on various sources for input. The present university belies the statement that an institution is the lengthened shadow of a single man. The president can persuade but he cannot make unilateral decisions. In large measure his persuasive powers within the university and his abilities to portray the institution to its various constituencies determine the efficiency of the president. His efficiency cannot be measured in terms of dollars and cents.

Decisions within the university come as the result of prolonged, sometimes painful discussion. Discussion must be prolonged, for a university is a complex organism within which no simple question can be asked and, certainly, no simple answer can be provided. Any decision has an impact upon many. Central university administration depends on recommendations from committees that in large measure are operating committees. The curriculum determines the majority of expenditures, and the control of the curriculum rests in the hands of the faculty. Recommendations from faculty committees cannot be summarily rejected and decisions with which a majority of the faculty (and today, the students) are not in agreement cannot be made. Such circumstances make good management inherently difficult. That it is not impossible of achievement is attested to by the successes of many institutions.

The university is not a production-line enterprise. There is no delivery to a university receiving dock of identical components to be pushed onstream through a rigid program to come out as identical products at the end of the curriculum line. Rather the university receives its student components with varying backgrounds, varying preparation, and differing aspirations. In order for the student to mature and develop to his own best advantage and that of society, a variety of options has to be held open for him. With the recognition that an undergraduate student's choice of career may change during his academic years, no rigid programing can be invoked to estimate space and faculty requirements. More careful programing can be invoked at the graduate level but even here unexpected changes are likely to take place. Whereas the corporation

THE USE OF UNIVERSITY RESOURCES | 49

can program with a great degree of accuracy, the same is far from true for the university.

Analyses of university managerial functions are difficult, if not impossible to obtain. There is for the university no profit and loss statement. Statistics can be developed to give an overview of university performance but none yet have been derived that give absolute figures relative to quality, efficiency of operation, or even relative success among peer institutions. The successful status of a university can be judged, in part, by the honors received by its faculty and the honors from extramural agencies bestowed upon its students. It may even be judged by the postgraduate records of its alumni, although there are those who believe this is a trifle presumptuous on the part of the institution; after all, if one starts with the best, one should do very well.

The fact is that one can truly tell if a university has won or lost only by reading the sports pages. Unfortunately, those results have little to do with academic performance (either of the university or the individual involved). Since this is a measurable performance, however, so far as interested alumni and friends are concerned, it is best for the university to have an acceptable record.

From the standpoint of university management, perhaps the most frustrating lack is that of an adequate parameter by which to measure productivity. Despite centuries of experience there is no formal mechanism susceptible to audit by which one can tell whether or not a university is performing as well as it might, or whether it is doing a better or worse job from one year to the next. The simple income-outgo statement does not suffice for this measurement. Neither does the number of degrees granted nor the number of credit hours taught per faculty serve to measure productivity. Relative assessments can be made within an institution or between institutions, but none of them tell the story as a businessman would want it told.

There is, of course, the crude attempt made to measure performance by establishing costs per pupil. The more complex the institution, the more difficult becomes the attempt to produce refined cost figures. A simple cost analysis that divides total expenditures by the number of students is a spurious figure not to be relied upon as any measurement. On an interinstitutional basis it has no meaning, for it masks the differences in complexities between institutions; on an intrainstitutional basis it has somewhat more validity, but there is only a rare institution that places any great faith in the substantive value of its figures.

Of primary concern to management is the efficient utilization of the physical space available to it. University management is almost overwhelmed by this concern. For certain subjects to be taught there is a requirement for specialized laboratories, so specialized, in fact, that they lend themselves not at all to utilization by other departments. General-purpose classrooms, of course, can be used by all departments; but it is exceedingly difficult to match classroom size, which is fixed by the dimensions of a building, to a variable number of students that register for specific classes. A classroom designed for forty is not used efficiently if it is used routinely for classes approximating twenty. Yet to build a substantial number of classes designed for twenty would be unrealistic. University management, therefore, is engaged in constant compromise.

Specialized laboratories that are necessary but cannot be used at 100 per cent capacity pose one difficulty for university management; but the library, which encompasses specialization and generalization and is used by all, poses by far the greatest difficulty. It is generally conceded that the library represents the heart of a teaching institution. Without it there is nothing. Yet the demands of the library made on university resources are inordinate if not insatiable. The number of journals continually increases as the magnitude of human knowledge increases. The number of books essential to complete coverage of every field increases each year, apparently without limit. Library expenditures become almost uncontrollable. To deny the purchase of needed volumes within a university is almost to be branded a book-burner. To deny the needs of the library is to run the risk of stifling scholarship. There are few managers competent to pass on the worth of a book or a journal; consequently, most of the requests are met, and sometimes to the acknowledged detriment of other programs for which funds are not available.

Finally, there are inherent limitations in university management produced by the customary method of selecting departmental chairmen, deans, and even presidents. Management's responsibility is to supervise and direct but also, more importantly, to lead. In the university, leadership is provided by outstanding scholars, the most productive men in their field. It is customary, therefore, to select the best man in a department to be its chairman, the best of the departmental leaders to be the dean. Thereby, management is likely to sustain a double loss; the scholar selected may lack managerial talent (although it is hoped he does not); the scholar turned manager has great difficulty in maintaining his scholarship—a good teacher or a creative talent may be lost forever.

In these days when the costs of education from the primary school to the university have become a matter of great concern, there has been no other function of the society exposed to greater continuing scrutiny. Government, trustees, foundations, individual citizens, all with a special concern as providers of funds, manager of endowments, or consumer of services have addressed attention to the spiraling costs of education. The university has felt the impact of inflation, the pressures of growth, and the effect of improved technology. Growth and improved technology have brought some of its facilities to the point of obsolescence; inflation has made the replacement of those facilities a difficult task to accomplish. Universities have engaged in self-appraisal, and they have sought advice from outside agencies. For no matter how unusual an enterprise is, no matter how successful its record of accomplishment has been, there is always opportunity to improve its performance.

Universities are corporate enterprises that function under the control of trustees. It is fair to say that in the past the position of trustees has often been considered an accolade, a sort of honor bestowed for past achievement rather than a post of responsibility demanding continuous attention. Many boards of trustees met on a semiannual or annual basis, heard the report of the president, dined with a few key faculty members, chatted with an occasional student, made a monetary contribution (rarely large enough), and basked in the prestige of their position. It was not that they had little to offer by way of advice and counsel; rather, they were rarely asked for it and they felt presumptuous in offering it gratuitously. A smaller group of their number, an executive committee, usually oversaw the management of the endowment and served as close advisers to the president.

These days are past. Trustees today must be workers if they are to fulfill their responsibilities. They must ask the searching questions and assist in seeking the answers. Their handling of the endowment must be superb in order to assure maximum growth as well as return. The trustee must become a part of the institution, aware of all its challenges and problems, and conversant with all the aspects of its function. He must be willing to contribute of his time and energy without question; he must only be careful that he does not interfere in the responsibilities of the designated management and not concern himself with the day-to-day operations of the institution.

Since physical facilities represent the most substantial investment of any university and represent the greatest nonrecurring expenditures, universities must engage in a continuous survey of space utilization, to ensure simply that class A space is being utilized for class A purposes. Such a survey must include all facilities: offices for administration and faculty, classrooms, and laboratories. It is a requirement that all facilities be utilized to the optimum.

It has been common to distribute space on a departmental or collegiate basis just as the responsibilities for curricular development were imposed in that manner. There should be little surprise that these units became semi-, if not completely, autonomous. They formed, at worst, individual satrapies or, at best, scholastic enclaves, oblivious for the most part to the needs of other departments or colleges around them. Many universities have solved physical problems by making the simple (and incontrovertible) decision that all space was university space and would be assigned on a university basis. In that manner classrooms and office space can be utilized to the advantage of the total enterprise.

In a similar fashion there has to be a continuous survey of the courses which are offered. Such a survey prevents a proliferation of similar offerings within separate departments and should avoid a continuance of courses that are either outmoded or superfluous. By the prevention of proliferation and the judicious pruning of courses whose day has passed, valuable faculty time is preserved, and usually a better curriculum results. Curricula should not be permitted to grow by accretion; they should be forced to grow by design.

Not surprisingly, it is occasionally found that entire curricula can be dropped or combined with other curricula in a meaningful way. Degrees offered can, in this way, be streamlined to the advantage of the student, the faculty, and the administration.

It is a poorly kept educational secret that graduate work across the nation is not of uniformly high quality. There are many institutions which offer the Ph.D. degree in fields beyond their competence. Neither their library resources, nor the preparation of their faculty make them adequate for such educational work. They are examples of the "me too" philosophy which is detrimental to educational quality. A great service would be performed in those institutions by forthright self-analysis leading to their withdrawal from such programs. It is often said to be easier to move a cemetery than to move a curriculum. That need not be true. Indeed, it must not be true if universities are to make the most of their income and retain their educational quality.

What is really needed to ensure efficiency of university management in conjunction with providing maximum educational opportunity for students is more interinstitutional cooperation. The sharing of unique resources in an effort to avoid costly duplication is a bright spot on the educational scene. It is evident that each university cannot provide every conceivable program and still maintain its budget within reasonable limits. Consortia of universities are now being formed to ensure this kind of economy. The Committee for Institutional Cooperation, the Mid-America State Universities Association, and others can be cited as effective examples.

This sort of interinstitutional cooperation began with a consortium of universities in the field of library resources. Those universities established a center to which important and unusual resources, albeit little used could be sent; any member of the participating institutions could then draw on these resources when they were needed.

It was appropriate for such cooperation to begin with the library resource, for, as noted previously, library demands are some of the most difficult to control in respect to university management. A great deal more remains to be done in this area and, fortunately, a considerable amount of effort is being expended. There must be literally miles of first-class shelf space devoted to the storage of little or rarely used volumes. When shelf space has run out, the answer has been to build a new and larger library with the expenditure of large capital sums. A much more efficient, and acceptable, method would be to identify the little-used volumes and house them in a less-costly warehouse facility, where they would still be available within a reasonable period of time, although not instantaneously accessible. There are not many volumes for which an interested reader cannot wait for a few hours or even a day. It is even possible for proximate institutions to pool their rarely-called-for volumes in a facility such as this. The average large university has accessions that annually require from a half mile to a mile and a half of shelf space for housing. No university can afford continuously to provide that much first-class shelf space.

Beyond the storing of little-used volumes in a warehouse, there are other methods available which, in the long run, could provide economies in library management. A great deal has been accomplished in recent years relative to the electronic retrieval of information. Even greater advances will be made in the years ahead. The statement has been made frequently that the best scholarship is produced when the scholar can leisurely browse or read with a volume in his hand. With the rapid increase in the rate of production of knowledge, with the consequent rapid increase in the amount of material available, it is quite likely that the day has passed when every volume can be made available for holding by every hand. Libraries cannot forever maintain traditional practices. Indeed, if universities are to continue to provide intellectual resources to their community, libraries must gear up to the present and, more importantly, to the future.

Similarities of University and Corporate Management

Although it is not usual to discuss universities and corporations in terms of similarities, it should not be forgotten that there are similarities between the two. The corporation, like the university, is a human creation. Its history is shorter than that of the university, and it came about for different reasons. It is, in essence, if it is successful, a creative entity. It engages in research and, consequently, adds to the store of human knowledge. It creates new products for the benefit of society. It has a social responsibility. A corporation develops and examines theory, and beyond that, puts theory to the ultimate test. It is corporate profit or lack of it that serves as the measurement of whether or not the theory was valid.

It is natural for the university and the corporation to exist in symbiotic relationship. Each is necessary to social and economic development, which will be enhanced if the two work closely together. In a larger sense, each is dependent on the other. The corporation depends on the university as the source of its personnel and leadership for the future, as a source of the continuing creation of new ideas and new concepts which can be implemented for practical utilization, as a continuing explorer of theory, as a source of consultative and advisory services, and as a provider of continuing educational opportunity for corporate personnel. The university depends on the corporation for advisory services and, most importantly, for continuing support of its operations. A healthy economy spurred by the success of corporate endeavor is beneficial to higher education; a strong university system ensures the future for corporate enterprise.

There is a history of fruitful cooperation between universities and corporations, some of which can be extended for mutual benefit by drawing upon the successful experiences of the past. To these extensions may be added new and previously unexplored areas.

Although the university cannot properly be described as a business, there are facets of its operation which are purely business-like and others that can probably be made more so. For instance, management systems within the university are in need of strengthening, in some instances, of establishment in others. Not long ago a corporate executive was discussing the fiscal problems of his alma mater. During the conversation he commented on the difficulty he had experienced in obtaining a meaningful summary of the university's financial problem. "One of the difficulties," he said, "is that the man in charge of certain vital operations is not a 'numbers' man." The "officer in charge" although not a "numbers" man was for many other reasons admirably suited to his position. What his alumnus could have provided him, in concert with others, was counsel without charge. But no one had ever asked him to.

Corporations could provide management counsel to universities on a one-to-one basis. In most instances, there is nothing more beneficial that a university could receive. This can be done in a way not competitive with consultant organizations of which, after all, there are surprisingly few.

There is one mechanism by which this could be accomplished that would be of substantial benefit to both parties. One of the most productive policies of universities is the granting of sabbatical leaves to faculty members. The faculty member, relieved of usual duties and responsibilities, is thus enabled to pursue his scholarly work in another environment. He returns to his post at the end of his leave, recharged with enthusiasm, possessed of new knowledge, and revitalized. It is surprising that corporations have not considered to any extent the possibility of granting sabbatical leaves to executive personnel. A man can go stale in his job. He can become less productive if he is protected from new ideas and new people. What he needs is not a vacation, but a working sojourn in an academic community. The corporate financial officer, granted such leave by his company, could teach on a campus, consult relative to management, audit a few courses for his intellectual advancement, and return to his position refreshed, renewed, possessed of new ideas and competence, with a verve for work. His company would benefit, and so would the university. There is a great deal to be said for cross-fertilization of faculty, students, and executives. Each comes away from such encounters with new respect for the other, richer for the experience. The executive sabbatical would be in the enlightened self-interest of the corporation and of benefit to the university.

In reverse fashion, there should be new opportunities developed for faculty members on sabbatical leave to spend their time in corporate surroundings. To the present such opportunities have been few. The value to a faculty member cannot be underestimated, whether he would study some area of corporate activity or work in a corporate laboratory. The more exchange developed between universities and corporations, the better will be understood their symbiotic relationship. A logical suggestion would be to develop between the two formal agreements for exchange of personnel, just as universities have developed such arrangements between sister institutions in this country and overseas.

There is another type of cooperative arrangement that has worked successfully. Those arrangements have involved work-study programs for undergraduate students as well as, in some instances, students at the graduate level. These programs are educational for the university and for the corporation. More and more it is becoming possible for graduate students to pursue their dissertational work in industrial laboratories. In most instances, these students are already employees of the particular company. There are, however, specialized corporate laboratories with sophisticated equipment that could be made available for dissertational research to nonemployee students.

Similarly, corporate employees with specialized backgrounds and talents have taught occasionally in neighboring universities. These programs, of exceptional value to the educational institution, can easily be extended for mutual benefit.

For years a substantial number of universities have conducted special executive-development programs, some for enrollment by executives from various corporations, some for enrollment by executives from a single corporation, some for enrollment by executives from special corporate associations. These programs have been widely applauded. There will be greater demand for them in the future, and more will have to be developed.

The future holds even more exciting opportunities for cooperative effort. Both universities and corporations show great interest in two of the most challenging opportunities: urban affairs and environmental conservation. A concerted approach to these challenges by universities and corporations opens exciting possibilities. The combination of urban planners and sociologists, experts in education from the university, and specialized corporate talents experienced in getting things done would do much to get the nation on the road toward success in solving the problems of the beleagured cities. Similarly, the combination of ecologists, naturalists, and engineers from the university with specialized personnel from corporations offers the greatest chance for protecting the environment and improving its status. It need not be said that either one can accomplish these tasks alone.

America is on the threshold of greater cooperative efforts and significant accomplishments by these two unique constituents of a free society, the university and the corporation. Their cooperative accomplishments will be limited only by the imagination of their leadership.

Campus 1980

KINGMAN BREWSTER

Someone once said the two capacities of a college president which are most indispensable are an infinite capacity for rationalization matched by an infinite capacity for wishful thinking. Forecasting in any field does depend more than anything else on whether the forecaster takes counsel of his fears or of his hopes, but there are a few things—three explosions, if you will—that are genuinely predictable.

There is the explosion of knowledge. This, for better or for worse, is the God-given human condition, a product of the curiosity of the human intellect and the capacity of the human hand and mind. Knowledge is bound to explode, and the explosion probably will grow at an exponential rate.

The second explosion, which is not inexorable but is for the near future inevitable, is the population explosion. And this does not mean only the birth-rate explosion. Because of the demands of society and the capacities that have been developed, there is also going to be a disproportionate explosion of what must be called the educable population of the country and of the world.

The third explosion is equally inevitable, not just because of external economics, but because of the economics of learning and research. That is the cost explosion. As new fields are brought into being, old ones do not necessarily die out. New costs must take their place alongside the old, as incremental costs. In the new fields, precisely because of their newness, there will be continuing fierce competition for talent, the scarcest resource in any business. And in the capital intensive field, costs will soar. That has already happened, of course, in physics. As the saying goes, it seems that the physicist is working on smaller and smaller particles with larger and larger machines. But this has its analogue in any field where systems, mathematics, mathematical analysis, and experimentation are crucial. The threshold of a social scientific revolution which tries to make comprehensible and manageable large corporations and large systems has already been passed.

Beyond these given assumptions for the seventies, much does depend on whether we do take counsel of our hopes or of our fears. If we take counsel of our fears, we will see a depressing if not an ugly situation. The university will continue to be a place where people feel trapped; where people will inevitably feel the tension between regimentation and the urge for liberation; and where, worst of all, large sectors of the university population will not be there for the right reasons and not motivated by the right goals. There will be an increasing student population which is unmotivated by the true purposes of the university. Students will be there to achieve credentials or to avoid the draft or because their parents insist they go when they do not want to. This population, being involuntary, will seek to manipulate the institution to alien ends.

Following the counsel of fear from the point of view of the faculty, one can predict a growing despair, which sometimes will take the form of mindless retreat and surrender, letting those who seek to steer the institution for topical or ideological purposes dictate the direction of the curriculum. If not capitulation, it may be a retreat into insulation from the university's life. The adult's counterpart of the "cop out," perhaps, is that faculty member who, despairing of the pressures brought upon him by the younger generation, seeks to retreat deeper and deeper into the catacombs of his library or laboratory, turning his back on the students.

This may well evolve into that kind of separation of teaching from research which often is mistakenly thought to be the answer to the students' needs; in fact it only insulates the research faculty from the pressure of a live campus. It was tragic to learn last summer that as a result of the internecine disruptions on Italian campuses, the Ministry of Education and many leading professors came to the conclusion that they should follow what is essentially the Russian and in part the German tradition of separating research into academies and institutes, leaving the university as a wholly teaching institution.

Harassed scholars, feeling that there is irresolvable conflict between the claims of students and the claims of the advancement of learning, would probably opt for the latter. This would be stultifying. Research cannot be stimulating without the stimulus of young minds, and teaching cannot be stimulating when it is not close to the frontiers of knowledge. Even when one is aware of all the difficulties involved, the American effort to have it both ways—to have the scholar a teacher, or the teacher a scholar—is one of the main reasons for the verve, the quality, and the progressiveness of American higher education.

If we follow the counsel of fear, the universities may become more politically vulnerable—increasingly dependent on political favor and increasingly fearful of political recrimination. At worst, that might mean political and ideological strings attached to government support in an effort to coerce the university along the lines of political popularity. At best, increasing dependence upon a single, public source of support is likely to impose that kind of conformity and uniformity which is the hallmark of bureaucracy.

These are not happy prospects for the campus of 1980. But before coming to what can and should be done, let us at least take counsel of our hopes for the seventies.

There is an obverse side of the fear that the campus is becoming a place where the student feels trapped rather than motivated. When the shadow of the draft is removed, not by an all-volunteer army, but by a draft system which allows a person to know where he stands before he graduates from high school, the draft will cease to affect his educational planning. At the undergraduate level today, everyone on campus is given a kind of sanctuary and a privilege by present draft legislation. The students themselves say that this is inequitable. The educators say that it is a corrupting influence in terms of the life of the campus, not because students are abusing the law, but because it keeps many on the campus who would not otherwise be there.

There should be a loosening up of the timetables, the schedules, and the escalators of educational progress so that each person has more options. People must be able to make choices which interrupt their education when for reasons of their own development it makes more sense to do so. What is needed is a realization that the university is not the right place for all people at all times. It is not the right place for all people some of the time, and it is not even the right place for some of the people all the time. There should be a break in the lock-step which has led parents and students alike to think that something is wrong if the path does not lead directly to college from school or through college in four years or directly to graduate or professional school from college.

Pressure is not the most important aspect of student motivation; some pressure is good for them, and it is still not too high. The great problem is excessive continuity. If a person is motivated by nothing more worthy than academic credentials from the age of five to twenty-five, he is being trained in a lopsided way. It is important to encourage students not to drop out or cop out, but to splice together nonacademic and academic experience. If we can develop an understanding on the part of parents, students, employers, and universities that education has to be to a large extent self-motivated, a greater contribution will be made to the quality of the campus and its effectiveness than by anything else that could be done in the 1970s.

Additionally, there should be in the educational experience more opportunities for second choices and clean slates. One of the problems of society, particularly with the academic society, is the increasing feeling that somehow at a very early age one passes a point of no return. Frowning on a second choice, a product of overspecialization and overregulation, belies the mobility, the quest for a fresh start that has been an important and unique attribute of the American tradition. Through opportunities for continuing education, for reeducation, and for late entry into the graduate and professional level, universities probably can contribute more to the revival of the fresh start than any other group or institution in the society. But this can be done only if universities make common cause with the central employing institutions, both private and public. If a partnership can be established with the employing community, if the inequities of the draft can be eliminated, and if the timing of educational schedules can be loosened, then that all-volunteer spirit which is essential to the pursuit of higher learning can be developed.

To the extent that multiple sources of support and multiple opportunities for the founding of new institutions as well as the moulding and shaping of old ones can be found, one can hope that the 1970s, rather than producing conformity, will respond to the explosion of knowledge. Hopefully the response will not be the imposition of some planner's blueprint but a greater burgeoning of institutional variety than has been seen before in this country. It is difficult to appreciate the contrast between the panorama of American educational life and higher education in almost any other country. The great significance of America's educational economy, like the great significance of its productive, commercial, financial, and industrial economy, lies not in its wealth, but in the variety of its initiatives. The seventies will demonstrate whether the nation's reaction to the knowledge explosion is one which proliferates variety or one which reduces everyone to conformity to the blue print of a single political planner. The outcome will probably depend more than anything else on the nature of the educational economy. If variety is the great hope for the campus in the seventies, then a greater variety of sources of financial support must be cultivated.

Obviously, in the great private universities, the nest egg of private endowment accumulated through the evolving generosity of generations of alumni, strangers, and friends provides opportunity for experimentation and innovation. Particularly in their scientific research component, universities will always be places where the enthusiasm of the intellectual imagination of the researcher and the enthusiasm of a sponsor—corporate, government, or otherwise—find common cause in the support of particular projects.

Another source of support which is at least as important as endowment, as far as furthering institutional independence is concerned, is annual giving with sufficient continuity to be relied on in academic planning. The hand-to-mouth foundation or corporate support, though welcome, does not begin to be as significant to an educational institution as a continuing pledge for three, five, or ten years. This is because there is more lead time required in the business of higher education than in most others. Time is not only required for tooling-up but for development of human potential which will take a considerable number of years to flower. A graduate student will not work in a particular field unless he is assured of support beyond his first year. If he is going to invest his career choice in higher education and research, he has to know that the support will be there for the term of his personal investment. Similarly, because of the tradition of academic tenure, it is essential to have funds for a lifetime commitment before an appointment is made.

Those universities which have been fortunate in developing the habit of annual giving on the part of their alumni know how much this means. The rate of giving to Yale University by alumni for current expenditures is about $4 million a year. Obviously, to the extent that the rate can be relied upon, a resource exists whose endowment equivalent would be enormous. In short, the impact of continuity in annual giving is almost as significant to the independence, the autonomy, and the capacity for experimentation and self-government of universities as the endowment is itself.

Continuing the optimistic projection, if the all-volunteer campus can be achieved, and if the dispersion of initiative and the capacity for innovation can be protected, the quality of the educational enterprise will not only be improved but in a very real sense it will make a fundamental, central contribution to the quality of the life of the nation itself.

Nothing is more central to the American heritage and the American promise than the widespread sense of personal choice. The central question is whether a society which increasingly requires and rewards organization and specialization can maintain a genuine feeling on the part of all citizens that what they do is to a large extent the result of their choice. This is never more important than in the motivation of those of college and university age. Those who feel that their plans and actions are their own, who relate success or failure to their own efforts, are likely to be the most dedicated and most constructive and least sour with the consequences of life. It is possible to have a society which is not only yeasty and colorful and creative but one in which people are not looking for scapegoats because they feel an element of self-blame in what happens to them.

A key factor is the shift in the universities away from the tendency to wrap all higher education into tight little packages. If one realizes particularly in an age of rapid intellectual obsolescence that the university must become increasingly a resource for a person throughout his life, then perhaps a sense of continuous questioning and the capacity for incessant change can be kept alive. The distinctive thing about the university is that one does not expect the person whom he meets next to agree with the person that he talked to last. Almost inevitably, an industrial organization, a financial organization, and certainly a political party, are built around like-mindedness and similarity of purpose among those engaged in the common enterprise. In the "calculated anarchy" of the campus, truth will be served best by an almost unlimited competition of ideas; controversy, far from being dampened, is encouraged. Agreement is never the objective.

Maintaining that kind of campus, but also allowing more and more people from the highly organized life of the society to return to the campus, serves a missionary function in keeping alive the best of values that goes well beyond what is measured in degrees granted or matriculants admitted. At stake is not only the kind of campus but also the kind of society America will have.

There are signs which justify optimism. The recent handling of the question of charitable contributions in the new federal tax legislation testifies to the fact that there is a lively belief in the importance to the country of the freedom of private charitable enterprise. Secondly, the ability of the President of the United States and his secretary of Health, Education, and Welfare to stem the tide of re-criminatory legislation which was rising in Congress during the spring of 1969 in response to student violence evidences favorable political leadership. Their effort was not so much prompted by patience with the students as it was against the use of the federal dollar as an excuse for extending federal police power.

Finally, the response of individuals and of the world of enterprise has given university leadership the courage to hope and the faith which justifies optimism. This country has a most unusual habit. Generation after generation, wealthy individuals, prosperous enterprises, and private foundations, built upon inherited wealth, have supported institutions dedicated to questioning the assumptions on which that wealth was made. There is something in this comparable to that unique invention of American constitutionalism —the independent judiciary. It is hard to explain to those from other lands how a country could be so perverse as to appoint, through the executive and legislative process, and support, through the public budgetary process, a judicial system which is then empowered to veto the legislation passed by the people who created it.

It may be said that the university and the corporation share a joint trusteeship symbolized by the many people from business and finance who play the stalwart, anonymous role of protecting the integrity of those whose resources they hold in stewardship as trustees of public and private institutions. But this joint trusteeship is more than the literal one of a board of regents or a corporation or a board of trustees. It is a trusteeship of freedom: freedom of the market, freedom of the ballot box, and freedom of ideas. That trusteeship must be seen in these related dimensions if America is to succeed in maintaining these three freedoms.

Growth and Change
in Higher Education

ALICE M. RIVLIN
JUNE O'NEILL

The most obvious fact about higher education since
World War II has been growth. Every year it involves more people,
more institutions, and more resources than the year before. Not only
has higher education been growing absolutely—like most things in
postwar America—but it has been growing faster than the rest of the
American economy. In 1940, there were about 1.6 million students
enrolled in colleges and universities in the United States. By 1960 the
number had more than doubled—to 3.7 million. Then, in less than a
decade, enrollment more than doubled again—to 7.8 million students
by 1969. The decade of the 1960s saw the most-rapid, sustained enrollment growth in the history of American higher education. Quite
apart from social and intellectual changes, just making room for that
many more students in a relatively short time was bound to create
strains and tensions.

Why are there so many more students? First, there are more young
people of college age in the population. The post-World War II babies, who were crowding the elementary schools in the 1950s,
reached college age in the 1960s. Second, a higher proportion of
young people graduated from high school and were therefore eligible
to attend college. Third, the proportion of high school graduates going on to college—a remarkably stable proportion for the first half
of the century—increased in the past decade. More high school grad-

The authors are members of the staff of the Brookings Institution. This article
draws on work supported by the Carnegie Commission on the Future of Higher
Education.

uates are going to college, presumably as a result of the rising income of their parents, wider distribution of college opportunities and student aid, and a growing realization that some kind of training beyond high school is necessary to a good job and a good life. And, finally, college enrollments have been swollen, not just by young people moving up from the high schools, but by older students staying in college longer or returning for further education.

These various influences on enrollment can be illustrated by comparing the academic year 1953-1954 with 1966-1967. Between these two years the population aged 18-21 increased 55 per cent; the number of high school graduates aged 18-21, 94 per cent; the number of undergraduates working for degrees, 155 per cent; the number of nondegree students, about 380 per cent; the number of graduate students, 200 per cent; and the total enrollment, 170 per cent. The spectacular increase in nondegree students is partly a reflection of the growth of two-year colleges, a phenomenon which will be discussed later.

Growth of Institutions

Along with the rise in enrollment has come an increase in the number of institutions of higher education. In some parts of the country, especially California, Florida, and the suburban areas across the nation, numerous new institutions are springing up. Many of them are public, junior, or community colleges (290 of them since 1960), but some are four-year colleges and even universities.

The number of institutions, however, has grown at a slower rate than the number of students. In 1953-1954, the Office of Education listed 1,871 institutions; by 1966-1967, the number had grown to 2,382, an increase of 27 per cent. The total enrollment grew 170 per cent in the same period. Thus the bulk of the increase was accommodated, not by founding new institutions, but by enlarging existing ones.

American institutions of higher education come in widely different sizes—most are small and a few are very large. In recent years, the number of small institutions has declined somewhat, while the big ones have been getting bigger and absorbing an increasing share of enrollment. By 1953-1954 the typical institution was small. The Office of Education listed 1,424 institutions (three-fourths of the total number) which enrolled less than 1,000 students. Almost a quarter of all students went to institutions of this size. In that year there were only thirty-four institutions with more than 10,000 students, and these also accounted for a fourth of the enrollment. By 1967-1968, the number of institutions with less than 1,000 students had declined to 1,167. Although nearly half of all institutions still had less than 1,000 students, these institutions enrolled only 8 per cent of the students. By this time there were 155 institutions with more than 10,000 students, and they accounted for 45 per cent of the total enrollment. The rising complaints of students about impersonality in higher education clearly have some basis in the fact that the typical student now finds himself in a large institution.

The resources used in higher education—faculty and staff time, buildings, and equipment—have all been increasing rapidly. Total expenditures (current and capital) of colleges and universities were about $3.5 billion in 1953-1954 and rose to $15.9 billion in 1966-1967. Part of this increase is attributable to inflation and part to an expansion of activities, especially an enormous growth in organized research on university campuses. The rest of the increase simply reflected the growing enrollment. After correcting for inflation, expenditures for instruction alone (not counting organized research and other noninstructional activities) increased during this period at about the same rate as enrollment. In other words, the surge of enrollment did not cause a decline in the real resources devoted to the education of the average student.

Higher education still absorbs only a tiny fraction of the national output, but the fraction is growing. Total expenditures of colleges and universities constituted about 1.2 per cent of the national income in 1953-1954 and about 2.3 per cent in 1966-1967. The relative growth reflects the increase in the proportion of students in the population, the expanding activities of institutions, and the rising costs of higher education relative to the overall price level.

Shifting Patterns in Higher Education

Although higher education has been growing rapidly, it has not been growing uniformly. At least in numbers of students and institutions, public higher education has been spurting ahead of private. Moreover, the role of private higher education seems to be changing and the line between public and private universities is increasingly blurred.

In 1900, almost two out of three American college students were enrolled in private institutions of higher education. Now almost three out of four are enrolled in public ones. But it should not be thought that private institutions' enrollment has been shrinking or even standing still. In fact it has been growing.[1] Public enrollment, however, has increased faster than private in every decade of this century except the 1920s. In the 1950s and 1960s the relative growth of public institutions was especially great. Between 1960 and 1969, public enrollment grew about three times as fast as private, with particularly rapid increases concentrated in public two-year colleges. The proportion of all students enrolled in two-year colleges shot up, rising from 15 per cent to 24 per cent between 1960 and 1969.

The number of public institutions is growing faster than the number of private ones. In 1968-1969 there were 1,476 private institutions of higher education (up 13 per cent since 1960) and 1,015 public institutions (up 44 per cent since 1960).

Private institutions tend to be smaller than public ones and the difference in average size is increasing. In 1969 the average size of public institutions was 5,556 (up 78 per cent since 1960) and the average size of private institutions was 1,438 (up 29 per cent since 1960). Within both public and private sectors, of course, there is still enormous variation in size. Universities tend to be large; public universities averaged 23,000 students per institution in 1969. Two-year colleges tend to be small; the average enrollment in public two-year colleges was 2,800.

Although private institutions' share of enrollment declined substantially in the postwar period, their share of total higher-education resources declined much less. In 1953-1954 private institutions accounted for about 44 per cent of both enrollment and resources (current expenditures plus capital costs). By 1966-1967, their share of enrollment had dropped to 32 per cent of the total, but their share of resources had dropped to only 41 per cent. Resources per student in private institutions had evidently increased relative to those in public institutions. Part of this relative rise is attributable to the big increase in organized-research expenditures in private institutions. Even if organized research is excluded, however, instructional expenditures per student (adjusted for price changes) rose in private institutions in this period while they remained roughly constant, on the average, in public ones. Evidently, private institutions were

---

[1] Note, however, that enrollment actually did decline slightly in private institutions between fall 1967 and fall 1968. The data for 1969 are not yet available.

offering increasingly expensive education to a declining proportion of the student population.

These trends are particularly striking for private universities. Between 1953-1954 and 1966-1967 the private universities' share of total enrollment declined from 19 per cent to 10 per cent, but their share of total expenditures stayed almost constant (22 per cent in 1953-1954; 21 per cent in 1966-1967). Real resources per student rose more in private universities than in any other type of institution; even faculty-student ratios increased while in other types of schools these ratios were falling.

Much of the explanation of rising outlays in private universities lies in the increasing concentration of these institutions on graduate education and research. In 1966-1967, one out of four students at a private university was a graduate student, compared with one in five in 1953-1954. Graduate education is more expensive than undergraduate education—sometimes two or three times as expensive—since it requires the time of experienced professors and sometimes expensive equipment. The concentration on research is even more striking. Private universities, as a group, now devote as much of their current resources to organized research as to instruction of students. In 1966-1967, total operating expenditures for organized research and instruction each accounted for about 37 per cent of total current fund expenditures.

Organized research is heavily funded by the federal government. In recent years the federal government has also extended other types of aid to both public and private institutions for student assistance, classroom construction, and other purposes. Most, although not all, state and local support still goes to public institutions. Mostly as a result of increased federal funding of higher education, particularly research, the line between "public" and "private" institutions has become somewhat blurred, especially for universities. In 1966-1967 private universities received 40 per cent of their total income from public sources (compared with 24 per cent in 1953-1954). One must ask in what sense an institution which receives such extensive support from the public is truly "private"?

Changes in Sources of Funds

With enrollment and expenditures of public institutions increasing at a rapid rate in the last decade, one might have expected to find a dramatic shift toward public funds as a source of support for higher education as a whole. Although there has been some increase in the public share, the change has been far from dramatic.

In the 1930s public funds accounted for about 40 per cent of the current income of higher education institutions. Most of the public support was from state and local government and flowed to public institutions. Federal programs were negligible. During World War II, federal government funds flowed into higher education for research, military contract courses, and other wartime purposes, bringing public funds up to 60 per cent of the total income of higher education institutions. In the immediate postwar period the federal share continued high because the G.I. Bill paid tuition for a large proportion of students. In the early fifties as the Veterans departed, federal support declined, but then picked up again because of increasing research commitments, and new student aid and construction programs. From the fifties to the present, this increase in federal funds was particularly marked in private institutions, where public funds increased faster than any other income source. Private institutions received a decreasing share of their income from endowment earnings and private gifts and grants.

Although state and local support expanded as enrollment increased, it did not increase as fast as other income sources. A decline in the average share of state and local support in public institutions was only partially offset by the increasing federal share. Public institutions as a group increased their reliance on tuition as a source of income.

Thus, despite rapid relative increases in public enrollment, there has been no marked shift in the proportion of total higher education income coming from public sources. Increases in tuition in both public and private institutions have kept the tuition share of total income roughly constant. Tuition, however, does not loom as large in the total higher-education income picture as it did before World War II when a much higher proportion of students were in private institutions. One curiosity may be noted with respect to tuition. Tuition charges per student have been increasing rapidly in private as well as in public institutions, yet the share of tuition in total income has not increased in private institutions. This seeming paradox would appear to be due to the declining role of purely student instruction activities in private institutions (particularly at the undergraduate level) and to the increasing importance of research with respect to both expenditures and earmarked income. Thus students, particularly undergraduates, are paying an increasing proportion of the costs of their education.

This brief review of changes in higher education, over the last few years, suggests some major questions about where higher education is heading in the 1970s. The answers will depend on the implicit and explicit decisions of the American people as to what kind of higher education system they want, how it is to be administered, and who is to pay for it.

How fast will higher education grow? The big population bulge which hit the colleges in the 1960s will slacken in the 1970s. The question for the future is: Will the proportion of the population (both young and old) who go to college increase enough to compensate for the lull in the population growth rate? In part, the answer depends on the future course of earnings and job opportunities for the college educated compared to those with less schooling, and in part it depends on how people view the noneconomic benefits of a college education.

As for the economic return, it is common knowledge that people with college training earn more than the less educated, and this is true even after taking account of all the costs of obtaining the additional training. Whether college training will continue to pay off is difficult to determine. Since 1950 relative earnings of the educated and the skilled have increased despite large relative increases in the supply of highly educated, skilled workers—a fact which suggests that changes in technology have favored the skilled. In other words, demand outstripped supply. But this may be a passing phenomenon. Indeed, during the first half of this century, as the relative supply of skilled workers increased, *relative* earnings of skilled workers fell and the supply appeared to outstrip demand. So it is difficult to say what will happen to the relative advantage of college training as the current graduates enter the market. Still another consideration is the argument that part of the earnings advantage of the educated person comes not from his education but from his greater initial ability. If ability differentials are responsible for most of the earnings differentials, then an expansion of the college population could lead to a lower return on the average and a much greater dispersion in the earnings of the college trained, with the newly enlarged groups of the less able earning a disappointingly low return.

As noted above, however, economic considerations are only part of the story. College also leads to direct personal benefits. If college education becomes more and more identified with the "good life style," it may be that as ability of families to pay increases, attendance at college will continue its upward course even if there is some drop in the pecuniary value of a college education.

Finally, changes in the cost of attending college can affect college attendance just as much as the economic or personal return. A large expansion in student subsidies, for example, could greatly increase enrollment.

What kind of institutions will flourish? Paradoxically, more young people seem to want a postsecondary education and fewer seem satisfied with the education they receive when they get inside the college gate. They complain that the curriculum is irrelevant, the atmosphere is impersonal, the professors are unsympathetic, and the administration is unresponsive to their needs. Although many reforms have been undertaken within institutions, no new model has emerged to provide an alternative to present college and university programs. Despite their diversity, American colleges and universities are still remarkably alike in courses offered, emphasis on credit hours, use of the lecture system, and other major features. A new kind of higher education may emerge in the 1970s, but it is not yet clear what it will be.

In particular doubt is the role of the two-year college. Will the public junior colleges which have been growing so rapidly in some parts of the country become a major feature of American higher education, and, if so, what role will they play? Will they become practical technical training institutions for all ages, or will they take over increasingly the first two years of the traditional liberal arts curriculum? Or will they try to do both?

Will a gulf widen between "first-rate" and "second-rate" higher education? Under the pressure of rapidly rising demand for entrance, most private institutions have become more and more selective. Those who used to take almost anyone who could pay the tuition now have serious entrance requirements, and the most prestigious undergraduate institutions are able to select from a pool of extraordinarily talented applicants—most of whom are also rich enough to pay the bill. Moreover, the most prestigious and costly public institutions are also becoming extremely selective. Selection of students with high test scores or a good high school record tends to favor those from upper-income families and good suburban high schools. The result is that students who already have advantages— intellectual and financial—receive the most expensive education, private and public, while those with less preparation, aptitude, and financial backing receive lower quality and less expensive education. Among the biggest questions in higher education in the 1970s will be: Is this track system acceptable and what can be done about it?

Who will pay the bill? Unless Americans suddenly decide they no longer value higher education, which seems unlikely, or unless some unforeseen technological breakthrough makes it possible to educate students far more cheaply, which also seems unlikely, it is virtually certain that there will be continued increases in both enrollment and outlays per student in the 1970s.

In question for the future is how these increases in cost will be divided. Will tuition rise in public and private institutions so that a larger share of the cost of higher education is paid by those who receive the benefits or will public subsidies increase so rapidly that a larger share is paid by state, local, and federal taxpayers? Will private philanthropy play a significant part?

To whom will the public funds be given? State-local support of higher education has always gone primarily for the support and operation of public institutions. Federal support by contrast has gone to both public and private institutions. Federal aid has also frequently gone directly to students. One important question for the future, especially if the federal government picks up an increasing share of the tab for higher education, concerns the form of public aid. Should this aid go primarily to institutions and, if so, on what basis? Or should it go directly to students—a procedure which strengthens the hand of the student in the marketplace of higher education and makes it possible to focus funds on students from low-income groups who might not otherwise be able to enter college? Finally, if either institutional or student aid is emphasized, will the line between "public" and "private" in higher education be further eroded? Changes in the extent to which higher education is subsidized and in the manner in which it is subsidized could produce dramatic changes in the entire fabric of higher education.

Financial Needs of the Campus

HOWARD R. BOWEN

American colleges and universities have made extraordinary progress in the past fifteen years. If one looks back to the early 1950s, higher education was in the doldrums. Enrollments were declining following the departure of the World War II veterans, faculty salaries were meager, capital plant inadequate and run down, programs static, the mood one of discouragement. After 1955, however, the nation was jolted into a new appreciation of higher education by events in Russia, especially the dramatic launching of their sputniks, and by realization that enrollments would soar after 1962 when the first postwar babies would reach age 18.

With this background, a new era of support for higher education was ushered in with mounting state appropriations, expanding private gifts, massive federal-aid programs, and rising student fees. It was during this period that corporate support became a significant element in college and university finance.

From 1955 to 1968, institutional expenditures for operating purposes increased five times, from about $4.1 billion to $20.4 billion. A dramatic increase in funds for support of students also occurred during the same period. This discussion, however, is limited to the financing of institutions, including only that student aid which is paid from institutional funds and excluding that paid directly to students from other sources.

In 1955, institutional expenditures were about 1.0 per cent of the gross national product; in 1969 they were about 2.4 per cent of the gross national product. Thus since 1955 the rate of growth in resources for higher education has been more than twice as fast as the growth rate of the national economy.

Many observers predict that the rapid and steady financial progress of the past fifteen years may taper off. It is often said that state and local governments cannot continue to increase appropriations at recent rates, that parents and students cannot stand periodic hikes in tuitions, that private gifts are approaching practical limits, that the federal government—busy in Vietnam and facing numerous demands at home—cannot provide rapidly rising sums for higher education.

At the same time, it is no secret that colleges and universities have been in a period of turbulence and that their popularity has been tarnished. They have been harshly criticized by some elements of the public and by some political leaders for student unrest, radicalism, and alleged extravagance. The general public, even including the best friends of higher education, appear to be less sympathetic toward the financial needs than they were a few years ago.

Yet despite the present stress, every responsible citizen knows that the colleges and universities are an indispensable part of the national life, and that civilization would not survive a single generation without educating new crops of scientists, engineers, physicians, nurses, lawyers, teachers, accountants, journalists, artists, and all the other hundreds of specialized personnel to keep the wheels running, or without the steady stream of new knowledge flowing from the academic world. Public leaders, though they are tempted to use the universities for temporary political gain, know that they must in the long run keep higher education strong.

The question that this nation must ask is: What are the *real* financial needs of higher education—the real needs in the public interest distinct from the views of those who would punish higher education for its alleged shortcomings and distinct from the wishful estimates of educators?

One assumption is made in this study, namely, that there will be no more general inflation—that prices will remain at the 1969 level. Of course, a discussion of financial need inescapably involves value judgments about the worth of increasing amounts of higher education as compared with other uses of the national income. No one has a monopoly of wisdom on questions of value but some of the underlying issues can be set forth.

Enrollments

A major factor in the rise of higher-education expenditures has been the phenomenal increase in enrollments. From 1955 through 1968, enrollments grew from about 2.8 million to 7.4 million of students, a nearly threefold increase.

Part of this enrollment expansion was due to the growth in college-age population. The number of persons of age 18 to 21 increased from about 8.5 million in 1955 to 14.3 million in 1958. Had college attendance increased only in proportion, total enrollment would have been about 4.7 million in 1968, whereas it was in fact about 7.4 million. Thus, 2.7 million young people were in college in 1968 because of increased college-going—because relatively more of them were entering college and also more were staying for graduate and advanced professional programs.

Estimates of the U.S. Office of Education indicate that the growth in enrollment is expected to continue throughout the 1970s reaching 10.7 million in 1977. Most of this projected increase is expected to be the result of more college-going rather than of population increase. By 1977, the number of college students will probably be about 64 per cent of all persons of ages 18 to 21.

The questions one must ask are these: Is it necessary or desirable for so many young people to be attending colleges? Are they all qualified? Would higher education be more productive if it did not try to take on so many students?

While answers to these questions are difficult, there are several relevant and persuasive considerations:

First, the figures include part-time as well as full-time students. When the enrollment figures are converted to full-time equivalents, they are reduced by about 20 per cent. Even after this adjustment, the number is still formidable.

Second, the figures on enrollment include not only students in four-year colleges and universities but also those in junior colleges and vocational-technical schools at the post-high-school level. Incidentally some of the vocational-technical programs are among the more expensive parts of the higher educational system.

Third, the expansion of higher education has not resulted in unemployment of graduates, though this result has been repeatedly predicted. The economy as it is developing technologically, seems to have an inordinate appetite for college graduates, for the products of various vocational-technical programs, and particularly for those with advanced study. Indeed, employers may sometimes place more emphasis on degrees and other educational qualifications than is genuinely required for the positions being filled. Yet the discipline and experience of college education is absolutely vital to many positions and an important asset in many more.

Fourth, careful studies show that investments in people, through college and university study, produce higher yields in increased lifetime earnings than investments in things. Recent careful studies indicate that investments in higher education are producing a return in enhanced income of neary 15 per cent annually.[1] These same returns are of course also increasing the national rate of economic growth.[2]

Fifth, recent evidence on the distribution of abilities among young people suggests that the capacity to do intellectual work at the college level is more widely distributed among the population than had been previously believed. Intellectual ability is deeply affected by family income and family background, and low ability is often related to life circumstances rather than to limitations of innate capacity.

Sixth, many of those who attend college do not receive degrees. The number of bachelor's degrees eventually awarded is only about half the number admitted to college.

Finally, the expansion of enrollment has not lowered college standards. Despite the vast numbers, intellectual rigor is generally higher today than it was, for example, two decades ago when the "gentleman C" was a badge of honor.

Thus one might conclude unhesitatingly that the expansion of enrollments to date has not been harmful to higher education, nor has it been harmful to society. On the contrary, beginning with the veterans, this expansion has contributed enormously to the national life, and the limit of fruitful expansion is not yet in sight.

The enrollment growth must also be considered from a political point of view. Young people and their parents increasingly are demanding access to higher education. Surveys show that families of all income classes are counting on, or at least hoping for, a college education for all of their children. Consequently it is politically inevitable

[1] Gary S. Becker, *Human Capital* (New York, 1964), 128.
[2] Cf. Edward F. Denison, *The Sources of Economic Growth in the United States*, Committee On Economic Development, 1962.

that society will provide broad access to higher education, access of a type that will give almost everyone the chance to try. This broad-based higher education will not be of one standardized type. It will offer varied experiences suited to persons of different abilities and interests so that genuine educational opportunity will be widely available, and academic standards in each type of education upheld.

A sound conclusion, therefore, is that the enrollment projections of the U.S. Office of Education for 1977 in Table 1 are reasonable, and that the nation realistically must plan for about 10.7 million by that year and perhaps 11.5 million by 1980. Clearly there are stresses and strains ahead, both financial and educational, in assimilating these large numbers. But the job has to be done. Incidentally, one aspect of the enrollment expansion that may disturb and sadden one is that the private sector of the higher educational system is not taking part. It appears likely that the future expansion will be over-whelmingly in the public sector.

TABLE 1

Benchmark Data on Higher Education, 1955-1956 to 1980-1981
(Assumes constant general level of prices beyond 1968-1969)

| | | | | Projected | |
	1955-1956	1958-1959	1968-1969	1977-1978	1980-1981
Expenditures (billions of dollars)					
Educational and general	2.6	3.9	13.4	27.4	32.8
Auxiliary enterprises and student aid	0.7	1.0	3.6	3.5	3.7
Capital	0.8	1.3	3.4	2.5	2.5
Total	4.1	6.2	20.4	33.4	39.0
Gross National Product (billions of dollars)	398.0	447.3	865.7	1,232.2	1,386.0
Total expenditures as per cent of GNP					
Educational and general	0.6%	0.9%	1.5%	2.2%	2.4%
Total	1.0%	1.4%	2.4%	2.7%	2.8%
Enrollment (millions)					
Total including part-time	2.8	3.4	7.4	10.7	11.5
Full-time equivalents	2.2	2.7	5.8	8.3	8.9
Population, ages 18-21 (millions)	8.5	9.0	14.3	16.7	17.1

TABLE 1—*Continued*

	1955-1956	1958-1959	1968-1969	Projected 1977-1978	Projected 1980-1981
Total enrollment as per cent of population, ages 18-21	33%	38%	52%	64%	67%
Educational and general expenditure per student (dollars)					
All students	929	1,147	1,810	2,561	2,852
Full-time equivalents	1,182	1,444	2,310	3,301	3,685
Professional staff (thousands)					
Total	334	403	775	1,028	1,100
Total, full-time equivalent	236	287	551	730	781
Total, instructional only	271	327	604	805	864
Total instructional, full-time equivalent	193	233	429	572	614
Ratio, students to professional staff (full-time equivalents)					
Total, all staff	9.3	9.4	10.5	11.4	11.4
Instructional staff	11.4	11.6	13.5	14.5	14.5
Average full-time faculty salary					
Current dollars (to 1968-1969)	5,500	6,620	11,595	15,129	16,532
1957-1959 dollars	5,895	6,573	9,335	12,181	13,310

SOURCES: All data (except on faculty salaries) for 1955-1956, 1958-1959, and 1968-1969 from various issues of U.S. Office of Education, *Projections of Educational Statistics*, e.g., 1968 edition, pp. 12, 14, 57, 62, 90, 92, and 120. Projections for 1977-1978 of enrollments, population, and professional staff, from same source. All other projections made by the author (see Table 2). Data on faculty salaries from Howard R. Bowen, "Faculty Salaries: Past and Future," *Educational Record*, 53 (Winter 1968), 10.

Cost Per Student

Rising expenditures for higher education are due not only to expanding enrollments but also to rising costs per student. If one divides total educational and general expenditures by the number of students, one finds that cost per student nearly doubled between 1955 and 1968. In 1955 it was $929 and in 1968 $1,810. The corresponding figures for full-time equivalent students were $1,182 in 1955 to $2,310 in 1968.

Cost per student is determined partly by the mix of students among educational programs of differing cost. It is determined partly by the market as expressed in salary rates and prices of construction, equipment, and supplies. It is also determined by what can be called the "standard of living" of the institutions. For example, salary expenditures will be determined in part by the number and qualifications of personnel employed. Building costs will be determined in part by the amount of space provided and by the standards of construction. Even expenditures for fuel and electricity will be affected not only by market prices but also by the standards of temperatures and lighting and by the hours that the buildings are open. Very little is fixed. The cost per student is not merely at the mercy of outside forces but can be influenced by institutional decisions.

One might go further and say that the biggest factor determining cost per student is the income of the institutions. The basic principle of college finance is very simple. Institutions raise as much money as they can get and spend it all. Cost per student is therefore determined primarily by the amount of money that can be raised. If more money is raised, costs will go up; if less is raised, costs will go down. Standards of operation as to number and quality of personnel, teaching loads, physical plant, and the like are set at whatever level falls within available income under the given market conditions. From the point of view of those who supply the funds, however, the question is: What are *reasonable* standards, taking into account alternative uses of scarce resources involved? What funds are genuinely needed to maintain an adequate educational system for America of the late twentieth century? These questions are often asked by governors, legislators, and donors.

One factor in judging warranted cost is the mix of students among various courses of study. For example, the sciences, engineering, and fine arts are more expensive than literary and social-science studies, medicine and dentistry are vastly expensive as compared with law or business administration, graduate study is more costly than undergraduate study, and so on. Also vocational-technical education is more expensive than freshman-sophomore liberal arts. The mix of students has changed since 1955. Vocational-technical education has expanded relative to liberal education, and the effect on cost has been upward. Undergraduate literary and social-science fields have increased relative to sciences, engineering, and the health professions, and the effect on the cost per student has probably been downward.

Graduate study has grown relative to undergraduate study; and within graduate study, science and engineering have grown more than literature and social studies. The effect on cost has been strongly upward. On balance, it appears that changes in the mix of students have tended in increased costs.

In the future, vocational-technical education will probably continue to grow as compared with lower-division liberal arts; graduate study will become relatively larger; and within graduate study, the sciences and engineering will have a place of rising importance. Little change is expected in the mix of undergraduate students. One field of study that must grow is the health professions, especially medicine and dentistry. The costs involved are fantastic. On balance, trends in the mix of students are likely to raise the cost per student, and these cost increases are warranted because of the need of society for increasing the number of vocationally trained young people, of scientists, engineers, health professionals, and persons with advanced study.

Grants, and loans to students are a rapidly rising part of institutional costs, especially as tuition, fees, and other college costs are rising and as colleges are trying to serve more students from low-income families. Much of the financing of students is being shifted from institutional budgets to federal and state scholarship and loan programs. This process should continue. Institutions have enough difficulty financing their programs and should be relieved of the need of financing students. At the moment, no relief is in sight. But many of the leading proposals for the future financing of education recommend that the government should provide for students, leaving institutions only the task of financing the educational costs. These proposals should be implemented not only to relieve institutions of an onerous and growing burden but also to improve the system of student aid and extend educational opportunity.

Size of the Staff

Higher education is a labor-intensive industry. The bulk of the budget goes to pay salaries. The size of the staff, both professional and non-professional, relative to the work load, is therefore a critical factor in cost. And within the salary budget, professional salaries bulk large.

Professional people are employed not only for teaching but also for administrative, research, and public-service activities. The need for professional staff depends in part, therefore, on the functions performed by the institutions.

In spite of the fact that colleges and universities have taken on a heavy load of research and service in the past two decades, the ratio of students to total professional staff has risen appreciably. In 1955, there were 9.3 students for each professional staff member and in 1968 10.5. These figures are based on full-time equivalent students and staff. Similar ratios between students and *instructional* staff show even greater change. In 1955, there were 11.4 students for each instructor, and in 1968, 13.5.

This record may be interpreted in several ways. One may argue that the increased student-teacher ratio represents an undesirable deterioration in quality of instruction, and that higher education needs a larger professional staff. Or one may conclude that higher education should not have taken on the extra research and service tasks and should have devoted more of its resources to teaching. One may even argue that if the number of students per teacher had not risen student unrest would have been avoided. Or one may argue that the rise in the student-teacher ratio indicates a notable and desirable improvement in efficiency. One hears all these interpretations. What is the truth?

On the question of research and service in the colleges and universities, one may be fairly conservative. Universities should not become involved in a wide range of applied research that could just as well be done by industry or government or profit-making research organizations, and they should not undertake service activities that can just as well be done by public agencies or by private consulting organizations. Universities, however, have an indispensable place in basic research and in public service, and their role in these fields should grow.

Research and service activities are genuinely needed in connection with the education of young people, and they are needed to keep professors in touch with the world. Even more important, universities occupy a critical role in the research and service facilities of the society. The university is the place where ideas are considered for their own sake and where there are few restrictions imposed by the need for practical results. This kind of basic, unprogramed, pure research which can best be conducted in a university atmosphere, is in the long run immensely practical. It is the source of most scientific and technological progress. It is also the main instrument for the advancement of culture in the humanities and the fine arts.

Similarly, the universities have a unique and critical role in consulting about new problems. Such problems are constantly emerging, and for their solution society has no place to turn except the universities with their large pools of diversified talent. As these new problems become commonplace, they are taken over routinely by private firms and government agencies. Meanwhile, still newer problems arise to engage the attention of the universities. In the years ahead, the universities are sure to be called upon for immense amounts of research and service relating to environmental, urban, health, and race problems.

The universities may be too deeply committed to applied research and to routine services, and some pullback may be desirable. But in the long run the involvement, if partly redirected, is not excessive, and it should grow.

Regarding the ratio of students to teachers, there is much loose talk about low teaching loads and underworked college teachers. It is true that in a few elite institutions, where there is heavy involvement in research, the teaching loads are low. And it must be admitted that in the academic profession, as in any other group, there are some freeloaders. But, in general, academic people work as hard, and often longer hours, than their counterparts in industry and government. Through careful management, however, it would be possible to raise the ratio of students to instructional staff without reducing educational quality. Indeed, education would be improved if students were given more responsibility for their own education and became less dependent on the guidance and supervision of their teachers. At any rate, the U.S. Office of Education projections show the ratio of students to professional staff rising from 10.5 in 1968 to 11.4 in 1977, and the ratio of students to instructional staff from 13.5 in 1968 to 14.5. This rise seems feasible. Certainly, there are at present many excellent institutions which are operating successfully at higher ratios than these. Care must be taken in applying these ratios to particular institutions, however, because the educational mission, the student mix, and the research and service commitments vary greatly among colleges and universities.

Facts on nonprofessional workers in higher education are scarce. Colleges and universities, with their great concern for adequacy of professional staff and for professional salaries, tend to skimp on non-academic staff. Secretarial and clerical help, laboratory technicians, teacher assistants, and administrative assistants are not employed in adequate numbers with the result that highly paid faculty and administrative people are spending large blocks of time on routine activities. Also, the physical plant staffs tend to be small with limited skills. As a result the maintenance of buildings and equipment is slack and probably in the long run costly because the stitch in time is often neglected. It is difficult to document these conclusions. The matter should be studied by management experts. But one may doubt if great savings are possible or desirable through reducing the size of the nonacademic staff. Indeed, an increase in the number of secretaries, clerks, and assistants may be one of the conditions of reducing the size of the professional staff.

Salaries and Wages

In 1955, the average salary of full-time faculty in all institutions in the United States was about $5,500. At that time, it was widely agreed that this level was too low if the academic profession was to attract and hold persons of needed competence. Great efforts were made to raise salaries to the point that the salary scale became a major index of an institution's excellence, and colleges vied with one another to present the highest possible salary scale. Since 1955, average faculty salaries have increased by 5 per cent a year, and in the past several years the increase has accelerated to 7 per cent a year, though much of this recent increase has been offset by price inflation.

The question is whether faculty salaries have reached an adequate level (taking into acount fringe benefits and perquisites) so that higher education can attract persons of sufficient competence. If so, then salaries need increase from now on only at the rate of salary increases for professional people in government, business, and the independent professions. If not, then more catching up is needed. A fairly detailed study of faculty salaries was made two years ago in an effort to answer the question. The conclusions were

that the upward surge of faculty salaries . . . has been highly beneficial to higher education and to the nation; that faculty salaries are approaching "parity" in the sense that capable faculty members are able to maintain a reasonable standard of living, and the academic profession is able to attract a reasonable share of the nation's talent; that the impending increase in the supply of new Ph.D.s and the increasing prestige of academic work combined with a slowing down in the rate of increase in financial resources will result in a tapering off of the rate of increase in faculty salaries. Barring inflation, I expect the annual increases in faculty salaries in the 1970's to be of the order of 2.5 to 3.0 percent rather than the 5 to 6 percent to which we have become accustomed in the past decade. I would caution, however, that the hard-won gains of the past decade must not be allowed to slip away through inflation or neglect.

The income of the academic profession from here on should at least keep pace with that of the society at large, and particularly that of the professional sector.[3]

Since the study was completed inflation has appeared and professional people in the colleges and universities are in danger of losing some of the gains of past years. Historically, faculty salaries have suffered from an inflationary period.

Concerning nonacademic salaries and wages, few data are available. It would seem, however, that colleges and universities have been on the whole low-wage, nonunion employers, and nonacademic salaries and wages have certainly not kept pace with faculty salaries and probably not with the outside market for comparable labor. Colleges and universities have traded on the attractiveness of the campus with its informality and its prestige and have also employed certain captive groups such as students and their wives at below-market rates. There is now a clear tendency for public and institutional employees to unionize and to become more aggressive in their demands. Students are no longer bashful about pushing their interests. One can expect an acceleration in the rate of increase in nonacademic wages and salaries during the 1970s, and well before the end of the decade colleges and universities will be paying full union scales with fringe benefits. Also, the last vestiges of exemption of college and universities from labor legislation will probably disappear. The cost is going to be substantial. The question is whether the increased cost will buy any gain in efficiency through attracting more-competent workers or making possible better methods and organization of work. Probably there will not be offsetting gains, and there may be losses because the new generation of workers may not be as loyal and faithful or flexible as the older generation. These conclusions, to be sure, are somewhat impressionistic.

The Library

The library does not claim a major share of total expenditures, but it presents a growing problem because of the expansion of detailed knowledge and the corresponding proliferation of books, periodicals, and documents. For example, the number of books published in the United States increased from 11,022 in 1950 to 28,595 in 1965, and

[3] Howard R. Bowen, "Faculty Salaries: Past and Future," *Educational Record* 53 (Winter 1968), 9-21.

the number of books published abroad and the number of periodicals have been growing apace. This flood of literature not only is costly to acquire but also to house and to manage. A great deal of study has gone into various ways of cutting library costs, including electronic storage and retrieval systems, microfilms, warehouse storage, and so on. But it appears that the printed word is still the most flexible and efficient device for presenting ideas and information, and the library will continue at least for the next decade to be the most effective agency for organizing printed material.

Education can become emancipated from the rigidity and narrowness of didactic textbook-lecture instruction only to the extent that adequate library resources and space are available. The most important competitor of the library as a means to greater educational efficiency is not the computer or the teaching machine or the audio-visual gadgets but paperback books which students and faculty can afford to own. The paperback book may be the most significant recent technological advance in higher education because it enables the student to be in part his own librarian. It would be a mistake to slow down the growth of library expenditures, and they probably will continue to rise.

Equipment, Buildings, and Maintenance

Equipment costs are skyrocketing because of the advancement of technology. In most industries, new technology tends to cut costs, but in higher education it tends to have the opposite effect. Electron microscopes, accelerators, computers, and renal-dialysis units are found today where optical microscopes, Bunsen burners, adding machines, and ordinary hospital rooms used to be. The new equipment often requires expensive space. It requires costly maintenance and technical attention, and it consumes megawatts of power. The equipment problem is more acute in major universities than in small colleges, but the latter are by no means exempt as they try to provide education fitted to the latter part of the twentieth century.

Equipment expenditures need close control. Among professors, sophisticated equipment tends to be a status symbol. Sometimes the need could be met at only slight inconvenience by using equipment located in other departments of the same university or in governmental and industrial laboratories, or in other universities. But even with rigid control, equipment costs will continue to rise.

Expenditures for buildings, land acquisition, and plant operation and maintenance are all escalating. Outlays for new plant expansion are about 18 per cent and for plant maintenance about 6 per cent of total expenditures for all purposes. The two together make up nearly a quarter of the total. This percentage would be considerably smaller, however, if the cost of the plant were calculated by amortizing the existing plant rather than by counting current expenditures for plant expansion.

There is no need to recite the fact that construction costs have been rising and will probably continue to rise. The real question is whether colleges and universities have too much plant and whether it is more elaborate than it need be. This again is a value judgment.

In rapidly growing state institutions, building space has not kept pace with enrollment; in slowly growing private institutions, space has grown more rapidly than enrollment. The great outburst of construction of the past fifteen years has probably resulted in a plant that is more adequate in both quantity and quality than it was in 1955. The gross square feet may not have kept pace with enrollment, but even so the plant is more adequate than it was in 1955.

As for standards of quality, there is no doubt that good education can be conducted in barracks, in quonset huts, or on two ends of a log. It is a legitimate question to ask whether graceful architecture, fine landscaping, air conditioning, private offices, and elegant interiors are needed. There is a belief in this country, inherited from Europe, that universities should be symbols of the highest and noblest thoughts and works of man, that they should become focal points of tradition and inspiration. Society should symbolize the importance it attaches to learning by making universities comparable in beauty to the best corporate skyscrapers or the finest cathedrals. All these things, however, can be achieved with simple buildings effectively sited and landscaped, even including some buildings designed for a short life. There is no reason for monumental structures or conspicuous and wasteful ornamentation on the campuses. Even so, both construction and maintenance costs per student are almost certain to rise in the years ahead.

Recent Campus Developments as Related to Costs

American colleges and universities are going through a period of questioning and reappraisal as a result of campus unrest and public criticisms. The outcome may affect cost.

On the one hand, colleges are accused of being impersonal; of using mass-production methods; of giving too little attention to teaching, especially at the undergraduate level; of being insufficiently concerned with such social problems as war, race, poverty, and pollution; and of giving inadequate opportunity to students from backgrounds of poverty and minority status. These criticisms are in part valid. To bring about correction will be costly. In particular, to admit millions of young people from poor and minority families, as the colleges are clearly being called upon to do, will be fantastically expensive if the job is done in good faith with all the remedial programs, special counseling, and placement activities that will be involved.

On the other hand, colleges and universities are accused of being excessively paternalistic, and students object to the dormitory housing, personal counseling, health services, supervision of extracurricular programs, and so forth, which have been traditional in American colleges and universities. Students are clamoring to be treated as adults and for the universities to get out of their private lives. It appears that many universities may be able eventually to reduce the traditional activities of deans, counselors, and housing and food directors.

The opposing trends may be partly offsetting, but the forces increasing costs are likely to be far more powerful than those reducing costs. In fact the costs of extending college opportunity and aid in rehabilitating our cities, cleaning up air and water, and improving the quality of life will probably be enormously expensive.

Economies

What are the possibilities of offsetting these increases by improvements in efficiency? Private business is often able to offset increases in wages and other costs by efficiency gains with the result that product prices can be held steady or can even fall.

In the past, higher education has made some efficiency gains—for example, the rising ratio of students to teachers. Also, there have been minor gains through increasing the scale of operation. But on the whole higher education has been unable (some say unwilling) to achieve significant gains, and rising labor and other costs have resulted in steadily advancing cost per student.

Most educators have grave doubts about dramatic cost reduction without intolerable sacrifice in quality. It is not merely ineptitude or conservatism or stubbornness that prevents higher education from achieving greater efficiency. Education is confronted by the same problem as other service industries like architecture or health care or barber service in which labor is the chief element of cost and the work requires personal contact with the customer. Education is a highly personal process which inherently requires large amounts of human time. Nevertheless, some things can be done, and educators have a heavy obligation to find any practicable ways to cut costs. Among the promising ways are: eliminating monumental architecture; building some short-term structures; increasing slowly and judiciously the ratio of students to teachers by increasing average class size; using low-cost personnel to assist expensive professionals; extending independent study; using teaching machines when they are appropriate; simplifying the curriculum; dropping unnecessary services and functions; and avoiding unnecessary duplication among institutions and cooperating in some programs with neighboring institutions.

These ways of achieving lower costs are all feasible and should be encouraged. However, on close examination it will be found that each

TABLE 2

Estimated Budgets for American Higher Education
(in billions of dollars)
(Assumes constant general level of prices beyond 1968-1969)

	1968-1969	Assumed Change	Projected 1977-1978	1980-1981
Assumes constant enrollment at 1968-1969 level:				
Professional salaries	5.5	Ratio of students to professional staff will increase from 10.5 to 11.4 by 1977-1978; salary rates will increase 3% a year.	6.6	7.2
Nonprofessional salaries	2.5	Ratio of students to nonprofessional staff will remain constant; salary rates will increase 5% a year.	3.8	4.7
Student mix	—	Increase in cost of 1% a year due to relative increase in graduate professional and vocational enrollments.	1.6	2.2
Library books	0.2	Increase of 7% a year in acquisitions and related expenses (not counting staff).	0.4	0.5

TABLE 2—*Continued*

	1968-1969	Assumed Change	Projected 1977-1978	1980-1981
Equipment	0.5	Increase of 7% a year to take account of technological change.	0.9	1.1
Purchased supplies and services, and other	4.1	No change, prices constant.	4.1	4.1
Construction	3.4	Construction cost will increase 3% a year; gradual reduction in volume of construction; gradual reduction in standards of construction.	2.5	2.5
Building operation and maintenance (other than staff)	0.6	No change; prices constant.	0.6	0.6
Student aid	0.7	Phasing out over the decade as other sources take over.	—	—
New programs	—	Increase of 2% a year to finance new programs relating to student affairs, minority groups, and social problems.	3.4	4.7
Economies	—	Reduction of 1% a year through improved efficiency.	—1.5	—2.0
Subtotal	17.5		22.4	25.6
Additional increase in budget due to enrollment expansion	—	Assumes enrollment of 10.7 million in 1977-1978 and 11.5 million in 1980-1981.	7.5	9.7
Subtotal	17.5		29.9	35.3
Auxiliary enterprises	2.9	Increase in proportion to one-half of increase in enrollment.	3.5	3.7
Total	20.4		33.4	39.0

one is of quite limited effect. With best efforts, the scope for warranted cost-cutting will permit reductions of no more than 1 per cent a year as an offset to the forces pushing costs upward. But this is a 1 per cent well worth striving for, and society can expect no less from the higher educational establishment. But even with considerable success in raising efficiency, higher education will require a steadily increasing share of the gross national product as it has in the past. This educational fact of life is a major source of stress and strain. It means that educators will be constantly pressed financially as they have always been in the past.

In conclusion, the needs of higher education in the next decade probably will be about $39 billion in 1980-1981, nearly twice the $20.4 billion of expenditure in 1968-1969, as shown in Table 3. This total increase would be about 5.5 per cent per annum, whereas the GNP is expected to increase at the rate of perhaps 4.0 per cent per annum.

The projected rate of increase, however, will not be as great as that in the period from 1955-1956 to 1968-1969 when expenditures increased five times. There is some hope that the rate of increase may be slowing down.

These projections are based on the assumption that there will be no more inflation. If inflation should continue and should average more than 2 per cent a year, as it has since the late fifties, then the projection for 1980 would be more like $50 billion than $39 billion. Fifty billion is two and one-half times the present rate of expenditure.

TABLE 3

Estimates and Projections of the Income to Higher Education for Operating and Capital Purposes, 1966-1967 to 1980-1981 (in billions of dollars)

	Actual[a] 1966-1967	Estimated[b] 1968-1969	Projected[c] 1980-1981
Student tuition and fees	3.1 (18%)	3.6 (18%)	7.0 (18%)
Federal government	3.5 (21%)	4.8 (24%)	10.9 (28%)
State and local government	4.6 (27%)	5.2 (25%)	8.6 (22%)
Endowment earnings	.4 (2%)	.4 (2%)	.7 (2%)
Private gifts and grants	1.5 (9%)	1.7 (8%)	2.7 (7%)
Income of auxiliary enterprises	2.2 (13%)	2.4 (12%)	3.5 (9%)
Other (including loans)	1.6 (10%)	2.3 (11%)	5.6 (14%)
Total	16.9(100%)	20.4(100%)	39.0(100%)

[a] U.S. Office of Education, *Financial Statistics of Institutions of Higher Education, 1966-67.*

[b] Division of Research, Council for Financial Aid to Education.

[c] In 1968-1969 prices.

If the total bill for operating and capital purposes must increase from $20.4 billion in 1968-1969 to $39.0 billion in 1980-1981, the question is: Where will the money come from? The task is a tremendous one, and all the contributors to higher education will be needed if the basic job of higher education it to get done. Table 3 presents estimates of the income to higher education for 1968-1969 and projections for 1980-1981.

Tax Support

The rapidly increasing demands for all kinds of higher education, accompanied by spiralling costs, inevitably raise the question of where the money to finance the expanded programs will come from. The first source cited is frequently the government, but before that answer is considered one should carefully examine the political and fiscal aspects of the possibility. What portion of the cost of higher education is now carried by the government, what levels of government, and under what administrative controls?

All levels of government in the United States—local, state, and federal—contribute to the support of higher education. The amount which each level of government contributes varies from one state to another. It would be safe to generalize, however, that the pressure on local taxes to support elementary and secondary education is so heavy that the proportion of municipal funds left for higher education is relatively limited.

Municipal universities, supported largely by municipal taxes, used to be an important force in higher education. But their rapid growth, coupled with rising costs, outstripped the cities' capacity to support them and forced most of these institutions to become state-supported. Local taxpayers were thus relieved of double taxation for public higher education in a number of cities.

At the county level, the growth of two-year community and technical colleges has resulted in some increase of taxes. Usually the county, the state, and the student have equally shared the cost of operating expenses. The state sometimes pays all capital expenditures; in other cases, the county and the state share construction costs. Even though there has been a substantial increase in the number of two-year institutions, many of which draw prime support from local tax funds, the per cent of local taxes contributed to them has not increased over the past twenty years.

Meanwhile, the nation's fifty states have increased their tax support of higher education. Chambers reports that state appropriations of tax funds for operating expenses of higher education totaled $6.1 billion in 1969-1970, up $1 billion over any previous year.[1] His figures disclose a 337 per cent increase in the last decade. North Carolina had the largest two-year percentage gain at 65 per cent, and Hawaii the largest ten-year gain at 742 per cent. Chambers points out, however, that "while state tax support continues to rise in actual dollars appropriated, it continues to decline as a percentage of total income at most institutions."

While the state governments were plowing $6.1 billion into higher education in 1969-1970—a 38 per cent increase over the preceding biennium—the federal budget recommended by President Johnson for fiscal 1970 called for $5.03 billion, an 8 per cent increase. But included in the $5 billion figure are $934 million for capital purposes (facilities and equipment) and $1.9 billion for student support. Other amounts include $538 million for institutions' current operations, including cost-of-education allowances accompanying fellowships, grants for libraries, health-professions schools, land-grant colleges, and developing institutions; $92 million for teacher training; $31 million for educational research; and $1.4 billion for other academic research. More recent calculations suggest that federal aid to higher education may be as high as $6 billion for 1969-1970.

To put the federal appropriations on a comparable basis with state tax support for current educational operations, it would be logical to subtract both the amounts appropriated for capital purposes and student support. Student support, it should be noted, goes directly to the student to enable him to finance his education. It does not, therefore, represent added income to the institution. The federal figure on a comparable basis would thus be $4 billion, of which the lion's share is for academic research. It is quite evident,

[1] M. M. Chambers, as reported in *The Chronicle of Higher Education*, October 27, 1969.

then, that the states finance a much larger share of instructional costs than does the federal government.

As a bench mark with which to judge the importance of local, state, and federal tax funds in financing higher education, let it be noted that the estimated operating costs of the nation's 2,500 colleges and universities for 1969-1970 will probably aggregate $15.8 billion in 1969-1970 dollars.[2] These are direct educational costs, not including auxiliary and ancillary enterprises or student aid or capital expenditures. Accordingly, state and federal taxes supply about 62 per cent of the estimated cost of furnishing collegiate instruction to some 7,750,000 students.

In noting the difference in the amounts appropriated by the states and the federal government for higher education one should keep in mind their distinctive aims and objectives. The federal government has historically looked to the state to finance public education. Indeed, as to higher education, the federal government did not participate financially to any substantial degree until the Morrill Act was passed in 1862, making funds available for research and instruction in agriculture and the mechanical arts. As the expanding nation was supported primarily by an agrarian economy and there was an industrial potential, Congress recognized the need to create and nurture agricultural, engineering, and technical schools.

The next big push for federal financing did not come until America was jarred out of its complacency by Russia's sputnik. There had been great reliance earlier on the colleges to produce officer talent for the armed forces through the ROTC units, and the armed forces used collegiate manpower in World Wars I and II through the Students Army Training Corps and Army Specialized Training Program respectively. University research talent also had been tapped by Washington for defense-related projects during and after World War II. And the federally supported G.I. Bill crowded the war-depleted campuses all over America as World War II ended. But large-scale federal involvement in financing certain aspects of higher education did not begin until after 1957.

Another motivating factor for federal financing was the desire of Americans for equal access to higher education. The states had provided free public education through high school for all, albeit the

---

[2] *A Fact Book on Higher Education* (Second Issue), American Council on Education (Washington, D.C., 1969), p. 9,106, with figures changed to 1969-1970 dollars by a 5 per cent inflation factor.

quality of that schooling varied from state to state. But as to higher education, state support in certain areas was so limited that high tuition charges often prevented talented but economically under-privileged students from entering college. The federal government stepped into the breach by supplying matching grants for campus facilities so that colleges could enroll and accommodate more students, and furnishing fellowships, loans, and paid work opportunities to enable qualified students to enroll despite lack of adequate family income. It is important to note that federal support was made available to both private and public colleges and universities whereas the state subventions, in the main, are available to state institutions only.

Nevertheless, the role of the state government is to supply the financial undergirding of the state university system. The role that the federal government has played so far is to utilize university talent and know-how on a cost basis to supply products and services the government needs, to aid the institutions—public and private—in improving certain teaching and research programs which the government might find of value to its economic health and military defense, to help the universities expand their academic and research facilities and student housing, and to aid promising but needy students so as to provide equal access. It is clear, therefore, that state taxes help to provide the essential ingredients of public institutions whereas federal taxes, up to this point at least, provide grants for special projects, funds for research, and aid for students.

Even though every university is eager to have funds for student aid, such funds help the student and not the institution. The aid given to students enables them to pay their student charges. While these charges cover a vital part of the institutional budget they constitute an average of only about 25 per cent of the operating budget for educational purposes. Unless there are matching funds which go directly to the institution for faculty salaries or equipment, student scholarships, fellowships or grants-in-aid add no new income to collegiate budgets. Indeed, more students usually create higher deficits for most colleges since the "selling price" is less than the cost of the educational service rendered. As the term implies, it is *student* aid not *collegiate* aid.

To understand the importance of state and federal taxes in helping to support higher education, one should consider the proportion of the cost of higher education borne by state and federal governments. The operating cost of the nation's 2,500 colleges and universities in 1969-1970 is expected to total about $15.8 billion. Using $5.8 billion from the states and the adjusted $4.0 billion from the federal government, the total of $9.8 billion accounts for only 62 per cent of the cost.[3]

Assuming that private support of higher education might reach $0.8 billion this year that leaves about $5.2 billion to be derived from miscellaneous sales and services, from endownment earnings, and from student charges.[4] The predominant amount must come from student tuition and fees. Collegiate endowments are estimated at $10.6 billion. Using an average of 4.0 per cent return, they would produce only $424 million annually. Less than 3.0 per cent of the cost of higher education, therefore, is covered by earnings on endowment funds. If the historical pattern continues, students will contribute almost one-fourth of the cost of their education; gifts and other income, including endowment, will make up the balance.

The Movement to Public Institutions

Another fact which should be considered relative to tax support is the increasing percentage of college students now going to public institutions. Table 1 indicates the trend. These data prove conclu-

TABLE 1

Student Attendance at Private and Public Colleges and Universities

Year	Private		Public	
	Number	*Per Cent*	*Number*	*Per Cent*
1939	638,250	47	726,565	53
1950	1,142,136	50	1,154,456	50
1955	1,180,113	44	1,498,510	56
1960	1,474,317	41	2,135,690	59
1965	1,915,693	34	3,654,578	66
1968	2,054,773	29	4,928,320	71

Source: *A Fact Book on Higher Education* (First Issue), American Council on Education (Washington, D.C., 1969), p. 9,009.

[3] The $6.1 billion state appropriation has been reduced to $5.8 billion since $300 million was allocated for capital purposes.

[4] *Voluntary Support of Education 1967-68*, published by the Council for Financial Aid to Education and the American Alumni Council in August 1969, reported $1.57 billion in voluntary support for that year, about one-half of which was for capital purposes.

sively that the enrollment trend is to the public institutions. Private college and university enrollment is up numerically but the percentage is down. As the trend continues, the need for increased tax funds for both public and private institutions will accelerate.

The rapid expansion of public collegiate enrollment can be attributed to the increasing number of public institutions, particularly at the junior and community college level; the academic development and scholastic improvement of public universities which increased state tax income has made possible; the enrollment restrictions of private colleges; and the lower student charges at public institutions. Of all factors, the last-mentioned is probably the most important.

As a larger portion of the age group aspires to a college education, a larger number of students from poor families seek admission. Many cannot afford the relatively high costs of private institutions. Moreover, the larger number of college students means that some families have several children in college simultaneously. Even moderately well-circumstanced families often cannot afford the high student charges at private institutions when several youngsters are involved.

The only factor which might slow down the effect of the concentration in public institutions would be an increasing tendency on the part of state governments to provide some aid to private institutions. The motivation to do so is not only to save private colleges from closing their doors but also to reduce the state's total cost of education. It would cost the states more to educate the students now enrolled in private schools if they were to apply at state universities.

There is a growing trend for state legislatures to appropriate funds to support private medical schools. For example, Wisconsin has appropriated funds for Marquette College of Medicine; Ohio, for Case-Western Reserve School of Medicine. Without state aid, certain private medical schools would close, thereby throwing a heavy burden on the state as to start-up and continuing costs, both for operating and capital purposes.

Another way in which state governments are trying to limit the shift of student population from private institutions is through instructional grants or tuition equalization programs. In some cases grants are made to students, on the basis of financial need, to enroll in the colleges of their choice. Certain plans favor private colleges since larger amounts are available from the state when tuitior charges exceed $1,000.[5] The purpose is to make it just as economical for a student to attend a high-tuition private college as to enroll in a low-tuition public university.

The federal-aid programs—grants, contracts, facilities, and student assistance—are open to both private and public institutions. If the federal government increases its support of higher education significantly and does not change its current policy of treating private and public institutions alike, the result will be to shore up the private colleges somewhat. Nevertheless when the important factor of state tax support for its own public institutions is considered, it seems logical to predict that the current trend of increasing enrollments in public institutions will continue.

The trend to larger proportionate enrollment in public institutions is revealed in these recent data: (1) Whereas there is a predicted total 2.9 per cent increase in fall 1969 enrollment over 1968, the public higher-education enrollment is expected to increase by 4.0 per cent.[6] (2) In 1967 public colleges and universities enrolled 64.5 per cent of all upper-division students in the nation, equally split between the public universities and the public four-year colleges.[7]

Prospects for Increased Tax Support

In speculating about the future support of higher education it is important to estimate amounts to be contributed by the two present sources of tax funds, state and federal. If the American goal of providing as much education as its youth are capable and desirous of obtaining is to be met, a larger percentage of the gross national product must be put into education. The President's Commission on National Goals in 1960 called for an increase from 4.0 per cent to 5.0 per cent of the GNP for all public and private education by 1970.[8] According to the Carnegie Commission on Higher Education, expenditures by higher educational institutions rose from about 1.0 per cent of the GNP in 1957 to slightly more than 2.0 per cent in 1967.[9]

[5] Instructional Grants Program, Ohio Board of Regents (October 1969), 6.

[6] National Association of State Universities and Land-Grant Colleges, Circular Letter, No. 28 (October 9, 1969), 11.

[7] American Association of State Colleges and Universities, Memo, Vol. 9, No. 14 (October 27, 1969), 2.

[8] Goals for Americans—The Report of the President's Commission on National Goals, 1960.

[9] Quality and Equality: New Levels of Federal Responsibility for Higher Edu-

Despite the 337 per cent increase in state appropriations for operating purposes in this decade, and the two-year gain of 38 per cent as reported by Chambers, there are grave concerns in academic circles as to whether state legislatures will continue to support their state universities as generously as they have in the past.

There are some disquieting signs. The cost of higher education financed by the state is rising precipitously as many major state universities develop graduate and graduate-professional programs. The instructional and research costs of these programs are many times higher than undergraduate-level programs. Yet there is no question of their need in the light of population growth, the greater sophistication of economic life, and continuing technological development. Twentieth-century society demands and absorbs more highly educated manpower each year. In addition to these higher costs, one must consider the continuing effect of inflation and the need to bring faculty salaries more in line with the compensation of comparable professions; the pressure of competing demands on the state tax dollars; the concern expressed by legislators regarding student and faculty conduct; and the fact that many states have already borrowed heavily for capital expenditures and have committed much of their current income.

The American dream of most fathers and mothers is to provide their sons and daughters with as much education as they can and will absorb. More and more parents realize that education for their offspring is a must, that it is the best weapon against displacement by the machine. They view education as the antidote to their youngsters' becoming "automation refugees." And, by and large, they want as much of the cost of higher education as possible to be borne by state and federal taxes.

As voters, such parents make their wishes known to their representatives in the legislative halls. But their voices are often muted by other constituents seeking larger shares of the tax pie. And so legislators are determined that students in public universities should bear a greater share of the rising educational costs. The National Association of State Universities and Land-Grant Colleges points out that tuition and fees increased in September 1969 by 16.5 per cent over the previous year. Public colleges and universities were

cation. A Special Report of the Carnegie Commission on Higher Education, December 1968, p. 6.

forced to increase student charges to balance their budgets when state appropriations did not come up to expectations. Some states have even tied the hands of university trustees and administrators on fee increases by legislative limits on maximum amounts which may be charged.[10] If this practice continues it may limit the development of state institutions so far as quality is concerned and restrict their efforts to expanding upper-college and graduate offerings. There is also a tendency on the part of legislators to erect more stringent "educational tariff barriers." The motivation here is that state tax dollars should be spent on the state's people.

Most states have always had some "educational tariff barriers." The usual method was to assess nonresidents a larger tuition charge or to set quotas on the number accepted. These trends have accelerated. With the specific aim of taking care of their own, many legislative bodies have reduced quotas of nonresident students admitted or have reduced or eliminated subventions for them. The latter device has required state universities to increase student charges, sometimes called tuition surcharge, for nonresidents, thus erecting a formidable financial barrier.

The validity of such practices can be seriously questioned. In some states the out-migration of students balances the in-migration. Others educate more nonresidents than the number they export. These are the states that might benefit financially from established quotas. Regardless of financial considerations, society can rightfully challenge the provincialism which results from such restrictions.

As a further check on enrollment of out-of-state students, some state university governing boards have imposed restrictions on the erection of new residential facilities, even though such dormitories can be self-liquidating and do not involve direct state funding. This practice boomerangs by limiting even students who are residents of the state from attending public institutions of their choice, forcing them to become commuter students at the college nearest their home.

All things considered, despite what legislatures have done recently for their state universities, one cannot dispute the assertion of the National Association of State Universities and Land-Grant Colleges that "while state tax support continues to rise in actual dollars appropriated, it continues to decline as a percentage of total income at most institutions." And the end is not yet in

[10] Substitute H.B. 531, 109th Ohio General Assembly.

sight. It is not comforting, then, to face the likelihood of a proportionate drop in the share of the cost borne by the states.

Prospects at the Federal Level

As previously mentioned, federal assistance to higher education has
been mainly peripheral aid to the institutions. In a sense, it helps
support the side shows rather than the main event. While it is an
essential ingredient in the total support of educational and research
operations, the fundamental philosophy and policy of federal aid
will have to be changed if federal taxes are to play a more meaningful role in financing higher education.

Adhering to the historic principle that education of its youth
is the responsibility of the state governments, Congress has not
appropriated funds up to the present to any extent for annual operating expenses of colleges and universities. The College Housing Loan
program, the Higher Education Facilities Act, and the help through
urban renewal have been a great boon to institutions to improve
their residential and academic plants. These special programs did,
as the federal government intended, enable the institutions to accept more students. But they also increased operating costs to which
the federal government makes no contributions; the institutions
now have to support enlarged facilities out of operating budgets.
The burden of support is passed on to the student in higher student
charges.

The federal government has, of course, helped some students carry
these higher charges through loans and paid work. But again, this
is *student* aid, not *institutional* aid.

In the research area, federal aid has essentially been on a cost-
reimbursement basis. The government purchases research services.
This does enable the institution to build up its teaching and research staff, but the colleges and universities then become beholden
to the government for continuing grants to finance their augmented
academic staffs. Where tenure is involved, this practice puts an
added burden on the institution.

Certain federal agencies have appropriated limited sums to a small
number of universities to build up academic and research competence. The National Science Foundation, through its University Science Development Program ("Centers of Excellence"), Departmental
Science Development Program, College Science Improvement Program, and the U.S. Department of Defense, through its Project

Themis, are good illustrations. But when the total financial obligation of the nation's colleges and universities is considered, these
examples of federal support, worthy as they are, have had only a
limited impact.

Those advocating increased federal aid are hopeful of some fundamental changes in the philosophy of support to colleges and universities. The American Council on Education, through its Commission on Federal Relations, is pushing for *institutional* support to
supplement *project* support by federal agencies. So is the Carnegie
Commission on Higher Education. If the federal government accepts this principle, there will be a fundamental breakthrough in
the concept of federal aid to higher education.

Institutional support would be of immediate, direct aid to financially beleaguered colleges and universities. It would begin to approach the direct aid of state governments to state universities. It
would supply, hopefully on an annual basis, some dollars to pay
faculty and staff salaries, and to cover maintenance costs. It could
be likened to the free dollars certain colleges have from unre-
stricted endowment funds. These are the most welcome of all dollars to collegiate administrators haunted by rising costs.

Assuming that Congress may eventually approve the principle of
direct institutional aid and that the church-and-state issue does not
vitiate the operation of such a project, this question remains: How
soon and at what amount?

Federal aid to higher education increased dramatically during the
Johnson Administration—from $1.5 billion in 1961-1962 to $4.8
billion in 1968-1969. However, that aid had definite restrictive features related earlier. The Nixon Administration is showing no
evidence of sponsoring another breakthrough in federal aid for
higher education. Indeed the reverse is true. The cutback in federal
agencies' grants for and purchases of research services has posed
dire problems for some institutions. Even the matching funds for
academic facilities and loans for student housing have been cur-
tailed.

Collegiate administrators hope, of course, that an end to the war
in Vietnam may free funds which can be used for aid to higher
education. It is reasonable to suppose that this may happen, but
the main question will be how much more higher education is likely
to get and what social programs will get the highest priorities. Massive sums will have to go to the cities, to health, to welfare, to the

poor, to air- and water-pollution control, to mass transportation, to highways. Will higher education rank high enough on the priority scale to get a reasonable share of federal aid?

The tax reform policy will have a great bearing on how much and what type of federal aid will be given to higher education. Ignoring specifics which may have great influence, it can be noted that there is a determination to reduce federal taxes. Will there be sufficient revenue to expand federal aid at the very time that there are so many other grave needs for the federal tax dollars? These questions are really unanswerable, but one can consider how much would be needed if federal aid were merely maintained at its present level.

In its projections as to annual educational costs, the American Council on Education predicted the 1969-1970 need of $14.3 billion in 1967-1968 constant dollars. When this is converted to 1969-1970 dollars, the need is $15.8 billion. In 1969-1970 constant dollars this cost will rise to $24.6 billion by 1977-1978.[11]

Assuming no change in the philosophy of federal aid, i.e., that it will be restricted as to use as it now is, the present $4.0 billion for current educational expenditures would have to be $6.2 billion in 1977, or a 55 per cent increase. Using similar projections, state and local aid would have to be increased from $5.8 billion to $9.1 billion by 1977, or 57 per cent; and student charges would go from $3.7 billion to $5.7 billion, or an increase of 54 per cent. With those assumptions, the current educational and general expenses of the nation's colleges would be covered as shown in Table 2.

Capital Expenditures

Throughout this paper the emphasis has been on current operating expenses. State and federal tax funds used for plant and equipment have been mentioned only briefly. But there is also a critical need for additional plant and equipment in most of the nation's 2,500 colleges and universities. To accommodate burgeoning enrollments, larger faculties, and expanding research programs, the facility requirements are prodigious. Add to this the vast requirements for space for rapidly developing graduate and graduate-professional programs.

[11] *A Fact Book on Higher Education* (Second Issue), American Council on Education (Washington, D.C., 1969), 9,106.

TABLE 2

Current Educational and General Expenses
of the Nation's Colleges and Universities
(in millions of constant 1969-1970 dollars)

	1969-1970		1977-1978	
	Amount	Percentage	Amount	Percentage
Student tuition and fees	3.7	23	5.7	23
Federal government	4.0	25	6.2	25
State and local government	5.8	37	9.1	37
Endowment earnings	.4	3	.7	3
Gifts and grants	.8	5	1.2	5
Other (including sales and services)	1.1	7	1.7	7
Total	15.8	100	24.6	100

SOURCE: *A Fact Book on Higher Education* (Second Issue), American Council on Education (Washington, D.C., 1969), pp. 9, 106-9, 107, with the author's projections.

Desperate as this need is, the overriding problem now is current operating income. There seem to be more new ways of financing additional plant and equipment, through bonded indebtedness and self-liquidating loans, than there are new ways of finding operating income. It is for this reason that the emphasis here is on the need to supply the annual income dollars to cover day-to-day educational operations.

Conclusion

Up to the present, the American people have pinned their faith on education. They have recognized what it has done in providing one of the important means of raising a young nation to the pinnacle of world leadership. At the level of higher education they have paid the increased taxes and furnished the tuition and fees, as well as private funds, to cope with the twin explosions of knowledge and numbers. Additionally, they have opened collegiate doors to those heretofore denied because of financial limitations.

Despite these great gains, it now appears that the American nation is facing so many grave new social problems that the percentage of tax dollars available for higher education may not be sufficient to assure the continued high quality of its academic and research programs. It seems unmistakably apparent, therefore, that an increasing flow of private funds—from corporations, foundations, and individuals—will be needed in the years ahead to assure sound educational opportunities for coming generations of Americans.

It will take a 10 per cent annual increase in private giving of all types to keep pace with rising demands for higher education even if state, local, and federal tax funds continue to absorb their present share of the educational costs and if student charges go up in like amounts. The critical areas are state and local taxes and federal subventions. If they fall off, the burden will have to be assumed by the student and by the private sector.

As the first president of the Council for Financial Aid to Education, the late Dr. Wilson Compton, used to say: "What happens to American higher education will ultimately happen to America." If all segments of American society recognize the overriding importance of higher education to the nation's safety and well-being, all supporting groups—the public sector, the private sector, and the students—should continue to do their proportionate part. The federal government, with its present more lucrative tax base, has a greater ability to maintain and even increase its tax support. State and local governments will have a more difficult time because their tax sources are not as favorable as Washington's. Unless private giving increases, the student or his parent may feel the crushing blow of higher and higher fees. This will be hard to justify in a nation which values trained intelligence and considers a college education for a large share of its intellectually qualified youth a social necessity.

Student Charges

JOHN D. MILLETT

The subject of charges to students for higher education is a complicated one. It raises far-reaching issues of college and university financial well-being; of higher education policy, program, and structure; of the student role in higher education; and of social purpose.

Various complications can be enumerated without difficulty. Should charges to students be defined as instructional and general, or should other charges such as those for room and board be included? Should charges cover a particular service, or be considered as general income available to the college or university for any purpose approved by the board of trustees? Should student charges be fixed at a single price or at varied prices according to the cost of the service received? Why should students be charged for higher education at all? This listing of issues could be continued at some length.

Regardless of the way the problem is stated, the search for an appropriate rationale for decisions on student charges which every college or university must make is by no means certain of finding a convincing argument. The fact is that, with few exceptions, higher education does derive considerable income from charges to students. Another fact is that these charges have tended to rise with rising family affluence and with increased demands on the part of colleges and universities for more income. Student charges are a present reality as well as a continuing concern.

This discussion will consider the subject of student charges from the viewpoints of the institution, the student, and the society, followed by an outline of an emerging postion which would relieve the student of some of the financial burden. It would be unrealistic, however, to expect that decisions on these charges will be made on any basis other than one of expediency for many years to come.

Institutional Interest

The latest data available on current income of institutions of higher education in the United States, as summarized in Table 1, indicate that in 1965-1966 tuition and fees—the definition of student charges for this discussion—provided about 12 per cent of total current income for public institutions of higher education and about 35 per cent for private institutions. For higher educational institutions as a whole, some 21 per cent of all income was derived from charges to students.

TABLE 1

Current Income of Institutions of Higher
Education in the United States, 1965-1966
(in millions of dollars)

Source	Public Institution	Private Institution	Total
Tuition and fees	892	1,867	2,759
Room, board, and other charges	1,181	907	2,088
Endowment income	37	319	356
Private gifts	191	547	738
Local government	311	8	319
State government	2,974	89	3,063
Federal government	1,429	1,332	2,761
Other	383	330	713
Total	7,398	5,399	12,797

SOURCE: Paul F. Mertins, Financial Statistics of Institutions of Higher Education: Current Funds Revenues and Expenditures, 1965-66 (Washington, U. S. Government Printing Office, 1969).

This sort of gross analysis, however, is almost meaningless. It shows only that institutions of higher education received nearly $12.8 billion in current income in 1965-1966, and that close to $2.8 billion of this income was collected as instructional charges to students.

It is far more meaningful to examine instructional charges in relation to the various activities of institutions of higher education, and in relation to the various types of institutions. The traditional threefold functional classification of expenditures of institutions of higher education is inadequate. Fortunately, the National Center for Educational Statistics has provided data which permit an analysis of income in terms of five categories of expenditure, as shown in Table 2.

TABLE 2

Source of Expenditures, Public Institutions, 1965-1966
(in millions of dollars)

Source	Instruction	Research	Public Service	Auxiliary Service	Student Aid	Total
Tuition and fees	846	1	7	20	18	892
Room, board, and other charges	18	7	112	1,043	1	1,181
Endowment earnings	23	6	1	—	7	37
Private gifts	66	82	9	3	31	191
Local government	296	3	12	—	—	311
State government	2,643	198	86	20	27	2,974
Federal government	420	895	53	7	54	1,429
Other	145	27	91	117	3	383
Total	4,457	1,219	371	1,210	141	7,398

SOURCE: Paul F. Mertins, *Financial Statistics of Institutions of Higher Education: Current Funds Revenues and Expenditures, 1965-66* (Washington, U. S. Government Printing Office, 1969).

It is evident that approximately 18 per cent of the total income of public institutions for instructional purposes was derived from student fees. One can observe from the data in Table 2 that relatively small amounts of income from tuition and fees were transferred to auxiliary services (possibly to support student health services and intercollegiate athletics) and to student aid. In connection with the federal government's support of instruction, it is worthwhile to note that most of the $420 million shown here undoubtedly went to the three military academies, the Coast Guard Academy, the Merchant Marine Academy, Howard University, other institutions in the District of Columbia, and certain additional federally sponsored institutions of higher education. If these federal institutions were omitted from the record, about 20 per cent of all instructional income of public institutions would have been derived from student charges in 1965-1966.

It is clear from Table 3 that close to 65 per cent of all income of private institutions for instructional purposes was derived from student charges. Sizeable sums for research were also obtained by private institutions from the federal government. Undoubtedly some of this income helped indirectly but importantly to support instruction at the doctoral-degree level, and undoubtedly influenced the graduate-fellowship matching grants for instructional purposes received by private universities.

TABLE 3

Source of Expenditures, Private Institutions, 1965-1966
(in millions of dollars)

Source	Expenditures					
	Instruction	*Research*	*Public Service*	*Auxiliary Service*	*Student Aid*	*Total*
Tuition and fees	1,803	—	22	9	33	1,867
Room, board, and other charges	9	—	71	826	1	907
Endowment income	253	7	27	2	30	319
Private gifts	397	71	18	5	56	547
Local government	1	6	1	—	—	8
State government	65	18	3	—	4	90
Federal government	140	1,143	13	1	35	1,332
Other	117	9	100	90	13	329
Total	2,785	1,254	255	933	172	5,399

SOURCE: Paul F. Mertins, *Financial Statistics of Institutions of Higher Education: Current Funds Revenues and Expenditures, 1965-66* (Washington, U. S. Government Printing Office, 1969).

An analysis of available financial data by types of institutions within the public and private groupings (universities, other four-year institutions, and two-year institutions), suggests two additional observations about income from student charges in 1965-1966: (1) whereas 20 per cent or more of instructional income at public universities and other public four-year institutions is derived from student charges, only about 14 per cent of the instructional income of two-year institutions came from student charges, and (2) whereas about 60 per cent of the instructional income of private universities and about 66 per cent of the instructional income of other private four-year institutions were obtained from tuition and fees, over 75 per cent of the instructional income of private two-year colleges was derived from student charges.

Little progress has been made as yet in the United States in the analysis of higher education expenditures and income in terms of instructional level: lower division, technical, upper division, baccalaureate professional, master's, graduate professional, doctoral, and medical. It is commonly known that there are variations in expenditure requirements according to fields and levels of instruction, but the magnitude of these differences is seldom known. More progress in such analysis has tended to be made in public institutions than in private institutions simply because the appropriation requests of public institutions are subject to close scrutiny every year or every other year by state-government budget agencies and by state legislatures.

Both public and private institutions of higher education seldom resort to differential pricing of student charges. To be sure, almost all state universities and state colleges charge much higher fees to the out-of-state student than to the state resident. The differential ordinarily is around 100 per cent. The justification for this policy is that the family of the out-of-state student does not pay taxes to the state where the student is enrolled. Undoubtedly the higher charge is also used to discourage out-of-state enrollment, which is often a political liability when state legislatures are reviewing state university requests for increased appropriations.

For the most part, both public and private universities tend to charge students the same instructional fee regardless of the level of enrollment or the specialized field of study. Sometimes the charge to medical-school students is somewhat higher than to other students, but the charge to graduate students is almost always the same as that to undergraduate students, regardless of expenditure differences.

Although there are many variations in practice throughout the United States, it is possible to generalize and to say that instructional charges to students at private colleges and universities tend at present to be above $2,000 for a two-semester academic year, while the instructional charges to students at public universities in their home state tend to amount to $600 for a two-semester or three-quarter academic year.

The Student Point of View

It may be accepted as axiomatic that students are not enthusiastic about paying the instructional charges of higher education. Until recently, very few persons considered the student point of view about student charges as of any importance. Today, very few persons doubt that the student point of view will have to be given consideration. But whether the student point of view will have substantial impact upon the financing of higher education remains quite uncertain.

For one thing, charges to students for instructional service are a time-honored practice in the United States. The early colonial colleges depended upon student fees for an important part of their income. Rudolph notes that the nineteenth-century colleges of the young American republic could not charge the full cost of instruction to their students because only a limited number could pay the charges then in existence and the colleges competed vigorously for this limited number.[1]

It was only after the Civil War, with the rebirth of state universities, the establishment of Morrill Act land-grant state colleges, and the creation of state normal schools that curricula became professionally oriented and the idea of low charges to students took firm hold as a means of encouraging youth to prepare themselves for new professions. State legislatures began to provide the operating appropriations to higher education which enabled state institutions to maintain relatively modest charges to students. And extensive philanthropy from those amassing great individual wealth in the years from the 1880s until 1930 permitted private colleges and universities to keep their instructional charges fairly low. As late as 1930 it was not unusual for the instructional charges of a public university to be around $100 a year, those of a good private liberal-arts college to be around $200, and those of a good private university to be around $400 a year. It must be acknowledged that at the same time faculty salaries were equally modest: $3,600 a year was a good salary for a full professor in a college during the 1930s, while $7,500 was a good salary for a full professor in a university during the same period.

It was only after World War II that many private universities discovered they were deriving more income from student charges than from endowment and gifts. Public institutions also began to increase their charges under the pressure of meeting inflationary demands and of competing for faculty members needed because of a rapidly expanding enrollment. The influx of veterans as students in 1946 and for the next five years, most of them drawing educational benefits under the G. I. Bill of 1944, enabled institutions to raise charges to students without much concern for their ability to pay.

[1] Frederick Rudolph, *The American College and University* (New York, 1962), 197-199.

As the veterans bulge subsided, the first systematic study of student fees was undertaken by the Commission on Financing Higher Education, sponsored by the Association of American Universities, and was published in 1953.[2] The commission pointed out that higher education conferred substantial benefits upon the individual students and that in the "reciprocal relationship" of student and society, student charges were "a valid source of income for both public and private institutions."[3] The commission also pointed out that per capita income and even income distribution by family units were improving even as fee charges were increasing.

Student charges have been criticized in recent years by certain students and others on the grounds that these charges constitute an economic barrier to access to higher education for youth from low-income families. If higher education is the avenue to upward social mobility, then individual ability should be the sole test of a meritocratic system of higher education.

Furthermore, it is pointed out that children of poverty families can gain access to higher education only if there is a massive provision of student aid which meets not only all the direct costs of higher education (instructional charges, room and board charges, books costs, transportation, and personal expenses) but also compensates the family for the income that the student would have earned if he had been gainfully employed.

To many other students, increases in instructional charges are an important personal constraint. Such students resent further financial reliance upon their families at a time when they are seeking to free themselves from parental supervision and to find an identity apart from their families. Moreover, many students today are likely to espouse personal behavior, ideas, and a life style with which their families are not in sympathy.

In any event, in 1969 there was an extensive student uproar about increased instructional charges by public universities in several states: New York, Ohio, Indiana, Wisconsin, and California, among others. The author is unaware of any student protests at private institutions specifically directed at increases in student charges, although it would be somewhat surprising if there have been none.

[2] Richard H. Ostheimer, *Students Charges and Financing Higher Education* (New York, 1953).

[3] Commission on Financing Higher Education, *The Nature and Needs of Higher Education* (New York, 1952), 123.

Certainly it seems likely that student reaction has become a new factor in the fixing of student charges by institutions of higher education, both public and private.

Students have been in an awkward position, however, to press a case for stabilized or even reduced instructional charges. To argue against such increases is to argue in favor of a reduction in the expenditures of higher education or in favor of an increase in the public support of higher education, either by government or by philanthropists. An argument in favor of a reduction in higher-education expenditures must sooner or later bring students in direct conflict with the interests of faculty members in improving their salaries. This is one conflict that students thus far have been reluctant to encounter. To argue in favor of increased public support of higher education is to acknowledge an obligation on the part of students to the existing social structure, the "establishment." This is an obligation that the militant student foreswears and the activist student has found embarrassing to espouse.

In the Soviet Union the student is an employee of the state. He is paid to enroll in higher education, and preparation for a professional career is part of a planned manpower program. This arrangement is the logical consequence of a totalitarian society. It is the functional requirement of a planned economy. But it is a proposition American students are indeed reluctant to accept. Ironically, it is the student charge which helps to underline the reality of student power on the American college campus and gives the student the financial right to claim a voice in the instructional operation of institutions of higher education.

The Social Point of View

The social concern with student fees is necessarily a dual one. It involves the social purpose of higher education, and it involves the calculation of means to achieve a determined social purpose.

Institutions of higher education, especially those where the faculties are widely recognized as teacher-scholars and have the most internal influence in shaping academic policy (and the two factors are obviously interrelated), tend to emphasize the role of colleges and universities as centers of intellectual discussion, where ideas and concepts are vigorously explored and debated, and where the individual is stimulated to the fullest realization of his intellectual capacity. This purpose is pursued for its own intrinsic worth, and intellectual achievement is its own reward. The idea that knowledge is power or that it has utility as well as personal satisfaction to the individual, is usually ignored or avoided. It might be added that the financial aspects of such a concept of higher education are seldom explored by its most articulate advocates.

Society is called upon to support higher education in a variety of ways, including philanthropy and governmental appropriations. It is properly interested in the social purpose of higher education, and this social purpose tends to emphasize the supply of educated talent to the professions of its economy. Moreover, in the past thirty years the American government has been critically interested in the research of American universities which may contribute to the objectives of national security and space exploration. The American economy has an interest in the instructional, the research, and the public-service activities of higher education which may contribute to technological development and growth. These social interests find expression in financial assistance to institutions of higher education in order to encourage and ensure the realization of these social objectives.

Institutions of higher education place a considerable value upon institutional autonomy, and desire a goodly measure of academic freedom in the formulation and pursuit of their goals.[4] On the other hand, administrative officers of colleges and universities, if not always the faculty members and students, are well aware of the need for social support and of the social obligations which that support inevitably carries with it.

The social concern with higher education poses some important policy choices in connection with the determination of the pricing of instructional services. Essentially these choices present two alternatives: (1) institutional support which results in relatively modest or even no charges for instructional services to students or (2) forms of financial assistance to students which make certain that no deserving student is denied access to higher education because of his income status.

In fact, American public policy has pursued both courses in the years since 1860, often in varied and even contradictory form, but nonetheless pursued. Publicly sponsored institutions of higher educa-

---

[4] For a careful recent statement of this value see Howard R. Bowen, "The Financing of Higher Education," in *The Future Academic Community*, ed. John Caffrey (Washington, 1969), 205.

tion were widely created throughout the United States by state and local governments. Fees were maintained at relatively low levels, and although these charges have been mounting in recent years, they tend to remain considerably below the charges of privately sponsored colleges and universities. The federal government has provided varied programs of student assistance (student loans, educational opportunity grants, work-study grants, and graduate fellowships), and state governments are increasingly providing student-aid programs (note the extensive scholarship program of New York state).

In large part, student-aid programs have been encouraged within the federal government and within state governments because of concern for the financial future of privately sponsored colleges and universities. But at issue has also been the question whether affluent families should pay a larger share of higher education expenses than the taxpayer. And equally at issue has been the urgent demand of institutions of higher education for more income. The one and only source of income under the direct control of an institution of higher education is the charge to student. All other income depends on the inclination of persons outside the institution: the executives and legislators of government, private foundation officials, alumni, friends, business corporations, and others.

If higher education is thought of primarily as an individual benefit, then individuals and their families may well be left to make a choice in the use of their financial resources as between intellectual satisfactions and material satisfactions such as housing, televisions, automobiles, and recreation. There is some evidence which even suggests that intellectual ability may be closely related to the economic status of a family, although no one would want to propose that there is an absolute correlation in this country between brains and wealth. It does seem clear, however, that the higher the economic status of a family, the more likely are the children to go to college.[5]

If higher education is thought of primarily as a social benefit, then society may provide increasing support to make certain that access to higher education is based on merit rather than financial status alone, that talent is encouraged to seek its fullest potential development, that the activities of educational institutions achieve the ends they are designed to serve, and that they are properly compensated for the contributions made to the productive output of the economy.

[5] Christopher Jencks, "Social Stratification and Higher Education," *Harvard Educational Review* 38 (Spring 1968), 277.

This social obligation may be met in varied ways, including low charges and financial assistance to students.

An Emerging Pattern

It has been observed recently that in terms of the economic costs of higher education, students bear the bulk of the expense, perhaps as much as three-fourths or seven-eighths of the total cost.[6] This statement is based primarily on the assumption that the student would be a contributor to the national output if he were not in college and upon the calculation of potential income not earned during a person's period as a student (perhaps extending from 18 through 26 years of age). The difficulty with this assumption and calculation is that it does not ask whether the student could in fact contribute to the gross national product. In the present economy of technology based on science the answer to this question is probably in the negative.

Higher education today is an investment in manpower similar to such economic investments as land development, the construction of plant facilities, the purchase of equipment, and all the ancillary economic activities from the growth of food and fiber and the extraction of mineral resources to the transportation and distribution of products. But here again the emphasis is on the social role of higher education in a complex economy. The fact is that the college and university graduate is essential to society and the economy, that higher education does provide talent which is in great demand, and the graduate is generally well remunerated for his contribution to the national output.

Regardless of the actual role that the student in the United States assumes in meeting the personal and social costs of higher education, there appear to be certain conclusions about instructional charges available from historical and recent experience. These conclusions may be outlined as follows:

(1) It is generally agreed as a matter of practical necessity and as a matter of institutional and individual considerations, that student charges will remain a major source of instructional income for higher education.

(2) It is becoming increasingly necessary to integrate the income

[6] Howard R. Bowen, *The Finance of Higher Education* (Berkeley, 1968), 7. See also Theodore W. Schultz, *Resources for Higher Education: An Economist's View* (Berkeley, 1969), a reprint from *The Journal of Political Economy* 76 (May-June, 1968).

and expenditures of higher education by such major functions as instruction, research, public service, auxiliary services, and student aid. Instructional charges should be used exclusively for support of the instructional expenditures of a college or university.

(3) There will continue to be a sizeable differential between the instructional charges of public institutions of higher education and those of private institutions. This differential will reflect in large part differences in instructional technology, especially in the student-faculty ratio.

(4) There will be increased attention by private organizations and by governments to eliminate financial barriers to higher education through student-assistance programs, especially through scholarship and grant programs.

(5) The alternative to student charges in support of instructional expenditures is increased social support of these expenditures, and this increased social support depends on the social obligations which higher education accepts and performs.

(6) Although there will continue to be instructional charges at the graduate and professional levels of higher education, more and more effort will be made to provide all graduate students with fellowships or part-time employment. To some extent these will be supplemented by loans.

It is time in the United States to recognize that graduate students must be self-supporting or must be provided adequate financial support while undertaking their graduate or graduate professional education.

Prospects for Voluntary Support

HAYDEN W. SMITH

Various bodies, public and private, have been looking into the question of financing higher education in the United States, and many of them have issued, or commissioned individuals to issue, reports and recommendations primarily designed to influence public policy. Most of these reports focus on the future financial needs of students and institutions of higher education and the probability of an inadequate flow of funds without new and enlarged programs of assistance from the federal government. Little if any mention is made of the possibility of increasing the flow of private gifts and grants; indeed, these studies tend to neglect completely the role of private philanthropy as a source of income to higher education. Yet voluntary support is as old as higher education itself in this country, and it has played a major role in the evolution of American higher education for more than three hundred years. Although its recent growth has not quite matched the explosive upsurge of institutional needs, its growth since 1950 has been phenomenal and for the 1970s the prospects are that it will grow much faster than college and university expenditures.

The History of Voluntary Support

Little can be said about the annual volume of financial support received by all institutions of higher education from private sources prior to 1910. The U.S. Office of Education did not begin to issue periodic statistical reports until 1870, and for twenty years the tabulated data contained no financial information. Although some data regarding income and property were collected after 1890, it was not until 1910 that the statistical reports included information on the amount of private gifts and grants received by colleges and universities. A clear picture of the growth of voluntary support is, therefore, available only for the last sixty years.

It is certain, however, that private giving to colleges and universities was a vital element in the financial picture of higher education prior to 1910. Despite the lack of comprehensive statistics for all colleges and universities, the records of individual institutions provide a graphic account of the importance of voluntary support both in the founding and in the preservation and expansion of higher education in the United States over a period of 272 years. Data compiled for the period 1893-1916 show that gifts of $5,000 or more to all forms of education amounted to over $1 billion; this figure is equal to more than 70 per cent of the total income of higher education during these years, and while the exact portion of these gifts going to colleges and universities is unknown, it was undoubtedly substantial.

Beginning with 1910 some information regarding the annual level of voluntary support of higher education became available, and with the passage of time it was more and more comprehensive. Even with allowance for changes in coverage and concept, these data, shown in Table 1, reveal a significant growth in the overall total of identifiable gifts and grants.

The tenfold increase in philanthropic support during these four decades is impressive, but the significant aspect of this growth is

TABLE 1

Private Gifts and Grants[a]

(in thousands of dollars)

Year	Current Fund	Plant Fund	Other Funds	Total
1909-1910	3,551[b]	8,379[b]	11,156	23,086
1919-1920	7,585	7,900	51,514	66,999
1929-1930	26,203	51,457	63,514	141,174
1939-1940	40,576[c]	22,679	36,366	99,621
1949-1950	118,705[c]	72,629	66,939	258,273

SOURCE: U.S. Department of Health, Education, and Welfare, Office of Education, *Digest of Educational Statistics*, 1968 Edition (Washington, D.C.) 1968, 95.

[a] May not include gifts of land, buildings, and other tangible property, or gifts specifically designated for student aid.

[b] Does not include gifts to separately organized professional schools.

[c] Includes the estimated value of nonsalaried or contributed services, primarily by members of religious orders; this amounted to $7.9 million in 1939-1940 and $17.8 million in 1949-1950.

that it implies a small increase in the relative importance of private giving in the context of an expanded higher education. The growth of private gifts and grants was faster than the growth of faculty, enrollment, and most other sources of institutional income. As a consequence, private support received per student increased from an average of $65 in 1910 to $97 in 1950; the ratio of total support to total faculty also increased by about 50 per cent in this period.

Voluntary Support Since 1950

Information regarding the amounts, sources, and purposes of private financial support of higher education has improved markedly in the past twenty years. The advances in this area are the result of an enlargement of the statistical activity of the U.S. Office of Education, and the direct surveys of voluntary support conducted by the Council for Financial Aid to Education (CFAE).

The amounts classified as private gifts and grants in the various accounts since 1949-1950 are summarized in Table 2. Aside from the inclusion of imputed amounts for the value of "contributed services" of members of religious orders, the grand total corresponds closely with the concept of voluntary support used by CFAE.

The growth of private philanthropy in support of higher education between 1950 and 1966 was nothing short of phenomenal. The grand total of gifts and grants in 1966 was 5.8 times the amount in 1950, implying an average annual rate of growth of 11.6 per cent. By comparison, the average growth rate during the forty years prior to 1950 was only 6.2 per cent a year. As was the case between 1910 and 1950, the significance of this rapid growth of support since 1950 lies in its relation to the expansion of higher education generally.

It appears that the growth of private gifts and grants between 1950 and 1966 was parallel to the growth of the overall financial requirements of the institutions of higher education. Again, the comparison is more meaningful for the components of private educational philanthropy than for the total. Giving for current purposes increased 12.1 per cent a year on the average, while the current operating expenditures of colleges and universities increased at an average rate of 11.0 per cent annually. Capital gifts for physical plant and equipment, on the other hand, grew at an average annual rate of 11.9 per cent, while the capital outlays of higher education appear to have risen by more than 14 per cent a year on the average.

Gifts for endowment and other nonexpendable funds have con-

TABLE 2

Private Gifts and Grants to Institutions of Higher Education
(in millions of dollars)

	1949-1950	1955-1956	1961-1962	1966-1967
Current Funds:				
Educational and general[a]	118.7	245.5	450.8	528.3[b]
Student aid	....[c]	22.5	57.0	91.8
Total current funds	118.7	268.0	507.8	620.1[b]
Capital Funds:				
Physical plant funds	72.6	143.2	226.5	355.7
Physical plant assets[d]	....[c]	....[c]	49.9	65.7
Endowment funds	62.8	186.2	230.2	298.0
Student loan funds	1.5	2.0	8.5	10.2
Other capital funds[e]	2.5	8.9	19.8	40.8
Total capital funds	139.4	340.3	534.9	770.4
Grand total	258.1	608.3	1,042.7	1,390.5[b]

SOURCE: U.S. Department of Health, Education, and Welfare, Office of Education, "Biennial Survey of Education in the United States," for 1949-1950 to 1959-1960; "Higher Education Finances, Selected Trend and Summary Data," for 1961-1962 and "Higher Education General Information Survey," for 1966-1967.

[a] Includes estimated value of "contributed services."
[b] Not comparable with prior years' data (does not include current-fund "grants").
[c] Not separately tabulated.
[d] Reported as "gifts-in-kind," not "private gifts"; it may, therefore, include some gifts of plant assets from government agencies.
[e] Consists of annuity funds, life-income contracts, and other forms of "deferred" gifts.

tinued to fall as a proportion of total voluntary support. In 1966 such gifts amounted to just over one-fifth of total gifts and grants. The cumulative book value of endowments for all colleges and universities was $8.8 billion at the end of 1965-1966 compared with $2.6 billion in 1950. Although the yield on endowment investment improved slightly in this period, the earnings from endowment in 1966 were only $356 million, a little less than 3 per cent of total current-funds revenue. This represents a further decline in the importance of this source of income in the financial picture for higher education.

Beyond 1966-1967 the only available clues regarding the further development of educational philanthropy are in the data provided by CFAE's Surveys of Voluntary Support of Education. From the data furnished by the institutions participating in these surveys, total support for all institutions of higher education was estimated at $1.57 billion in 1967-1968 versus $1.40 billion in 1964-1965, an increase of only 3.9 per cent a year for the three-year period. It is clear that the growth of voluntary support has been slower in the period since 1964-1965 than it was in prior years. With the possible exception of 1968-1969, for which information is incomplete, the percentage increases in every year since 1964-1965 have been smaller than the average growth rate in prior years.

This slowing in the growth of voluntary support is particularly serious for two reasons. The first is that the growth of financial requirements of institutions of higher education has accelerated sharply since 1963-1964. The second is that there are signs of resistance to accelerated growth in respect to the other major sources of college and university income.

The problems associated with other sources of income are discussed in other papers in this book. It is clear, however, that colleges and universities are encountering increasing difficulty in raising tuition and other student fees, in obtaining accelerated increases in state and local government appropriations, and in persuading the federal government to expand its financial assistance to institutional budgets. The need for an increased growth of voluntary support is thus imperative. The prospects in this area vary somewhat as between different sources, and it is necessary to examine each of these in detail.

Sources and Purposes

The outstanding feature of the growth of voluntary support since 1955 is that the percentage distribution by source has been fairly stable. With only a few exceptions, the relative importance of the various groups of donors has fluctuated within a narrow range, and the trends of growth for the support provided by these groups have all been roughly the same as for the total. The details are given in Table 3, which shows the amounts reported by the colleges and universities participating in the various surveys.

Individual donors have consistently been the largest single source of voluntary support, acounting for between 44 per cent and 49 per cent of the total. Next in importance to individuals are the general-welfare foundations whose educational grants have aggregated about

TABLE 3

Voluntary Support by Source
(in millions of dollars)

Source	1954-1955	1960-1961	1965-1966	1967-1968
Alumni	67.8	174.9	265.6	307.5
	23.4%	21.8%	21.5%	22.4%
Nonalumni individuals	71.9	180.3	299.9	349.5
	24.8%	22.5%	24.3%	25.5%
General welfare foundations	50.2	195.5	304.1	321.0
	17.4%	24.3%	24.8%	23.4%
Business corporations	39.4	131.1	195.7	213.8
	13.6%	16.3%	16.0%	15.6%
Religious denominations	26.2	73.5	92.6	102.0
	9.1%	9.1%	7.5%	7.4%
Nonalumni, nonchurch groups	18.7	30.5	59.1	60.7
	6.4%	3.8%	4.9%	4.4%
Other Sources	15.3	17.3	12.8	17.1
	5.3%	2.2%	1.0%	1.3%
Total	289.5	803.0	1,229.8	1,371.6
	100.0%	100.0%	100.0%	100.0%

SOURCE: *Voluntary Support of Education, 1967-1968,* Council for Finanical Aid to Education.
NOTE: Detail does not necessarily add to total because of rounding.

one-fourth of the total support. These grants, however, have fluctuated more widely, both in dollars and in percentage than the support received from other sources.

Corporate contributions to institutions of higher education, including gifts and grants by corporate foundations, have regularly constituted between 14 per cent and 17 per cent of total voluntary support. There is some evidence of a slight increase in the relative importance of support from the business community—it averaged 14.5 per cent of the total from 1955 to 1959, and 16.1 per cent from 1966 to 1968. This improvement is confirmed by other data which show that corporate contributions to education have grown more rapidly since 1958 than total voluntary support.[1]

Among the remaining sources of voluntary support, grants from religious denominations are most noteworthy. These include support from official church bodies, church auxiliaries, church service groups,

[1] *1968 Survey of Corporation Support of Higher Education,* Council for Financial Aid to Education, New York, 1969, p. 25.

and cash contributions from members of religious orders. Support from these sources has been relatively stable at about 7.5 per cent of the total since 1965. This represents a slight decline from previous years when it varied from 9 to 10 per cent.

Other sources not included above represent a variety of associations, service clubs, fund-raising groups, and other organizations and institutions not falling in any of the five categories above. These diverse sources accounted for nearly 11 per cent of total voluntary support during the 1950s; since 1960-1961, their share has been close to 6 per cent in all survey years.

One of the fundamental divisions of educational philanthropy is support for current operations versus support for capital purposes. The most significant observation about these trends is that while gifts for endowment and for other capital purposes dominated the support picture in the early years, gifts for current operations increased in importance until 1949-1950 when they amounted to roughly 46 per cent of the total. Since then current support has continued to account for just slightly less than half of all private gifts and grants.

It thus appears that, for all sources combined, there is now no great preference between current and capital gifts. Funds are needed for both purposes, and the inclinations of the various groups of donors, the mechanisms of fund-raising, and other factors all operate to make voluntary support responsive to both needs on roughly an equal basis.

Distribution of Support Among Institutions

Educational philanthropy may have as one of its aims not only a functional purpose but also the support of a particular type of institution. One of the major dimensions of voluntary support is, indeed, the distribution of private funds among colleges and universities which differ in terms of control, level of instruction, enrollment, type of program, and other factors.

Perhaps the most significant fact in this picture is the heavy concentration of support in a class of schools that is relatively small in number. The major private universities comprise less than 6 per cent of the reporting institutions, yet they and the types of programs offered are so highly regarded as to attract roughly two out of every five dollars of private financial support of all higher education. Although the proportion of support accounted for by this category has been as high as 44 per cent and as low as 36 per cent, there is no apparent trend in the included period of time. The large fluctuations around the 40 per cent level are easily explained by changes in the number of institutions reporting and by the inherent "lumpiness" of large gifts, grants, and bequests.

The share of total support received by private coeducational colleges, on the other hand, does appear to be in a declining trend. Between 1958-1959 and 1964-1965, this share fluctuated between 22 per cent and 25 per cent; in the past three survey years, it declined to 20 per cent. There is a similar trend in the data for men's and women's colleges; these groups of colleges together accounted for between 10 per cent and 12 per cent of the total until the last two survey years when their share fell below 10 per cent.

Private professional and specialized schools have had a highly volatile experience with voluntary support, both in total dollars and as a proportion of the total. Part of this is due to the periodic reclassification of major institutes of technology to private universities as a result of a broadening of their programs. In view of the decline in the number of schools in this category, however, the trend is perhaps best described as flat.

The share of total voluntary support accounted for by all private universities and four-year colleges combined has clearly fallen since 1965. In the period between 1958-1959 and 1964-1965, these institutions received 82 per cent or more of the total. In 1965-1966, their proportion fell to 78 per cent, and, while it rose to 81 per cent in 1967-1968, it remains lower than in any of the earlier years.

The publicly controlled four-year institutions, on the other hand, have increased their share of private educational philanthropy from an average of about 16 per cent in the 1950s to about 18 per cent in the 1960s. The evidence indicates, therefore, that, while the private four-year institutions consistently receive about four-fifths of total voluntary support, the growth of support for public schools has been somewhat faster than that for private institutions. It should be noted that this holds true for the past decade in spite of a modest reverse shift in favor of private schools in the two most recent years.

The voluntary support of two-year institutions has been small in relation to the total—between 1 and 2 per cent in all years. Roughly three-fifths of the junior colleges participating in past surveys are privately controlled, but they account for between 70 per cent and 90 per cent of all the support received by two-year schools, or about the same proportion, on the average, as holds for the senior institutions.

Other Factors

For any individual educational institution, its success in raising funds from voluntary sources depends on the skill and effort applied to its development program, the resources available to its potential benefactors, and the competing appeals to potential donors from other recipients of philanthropic support. To the extent that there is competition for the available support among colleges and universities, this factor drops out completely when one considers the factors which affect the total of voluntary support for all institutions of higher education.

In an analytical sense, the growth of voluntary support for all higher education reflects the growth of resources available to the various groups of donors, the changes in the proportions of those resources that each donor group collectively is willing to devote to philanthropy, and the variations in the ways in which these groups are induced to distribute their philanthropic dollars among the many causes appealing for funds. The available data suggest that the first of these factors is by far the most important in explaining the growth of educational support; the proportions of their resources that donor groups are willing to give have been generally quite stable, and the distribution of total philanthropy among major categories of recipients has changed only within narrow limits.

Ideally, potential resources for philanthropic purposes should be measured in terms of both wealth and income. In the absence of any usuable data on wealth, the only suitable and meaningful measure is income. For the nation, national income is the appropriate concept.

Between 1950 and 1968 the percentage growth of philanthropy was obviously much more closely related to the growth of national income than to the increase in the proportion of income which the nation allocates to philanthropy. Indeed, since 1960 the share of income given over to philanthropic uses declined slightly, so that all of the growth in philanthropic giving in the last eight years is "explained" by the growth of national income. It should be noted that the variation in the ratio of philanthropy to national income has been small; since 1955, this ratio, expressed as a percentage, has ranged from a low of 2.11 to a high of 2.41. By comparison to 1950, however, this ratio was significantly higher in the 1960s. This result may be attributed wholly to foundations and business corporations; the picture for individuals is one of great stability.

Contributions and gifts by living individuals constitute the bulk of total private philanthropy. This source of funds accounted for 87 per cent of all philanthropic giving in 1950 and between 75 per cent and 80 per cent during the 1960s. Such giving amounted to $12.1 billion in 1968, compared to $3.9 billion in 1950; the indicated increase amounts to about 210 per cent. This growth is almost entirely explained by the rise of personal income, which was 202 per cent during these years.

Philanthropic giving by bequest also exhibits a high degree of stability in terms of the resources available for distribution. Information regarding this area is less complete than for other sources of gifts, but is sufficient for at least a tentative conclusion. The growth of charitable bequests is clearly due much more to an increase in the total value of estates reported in estate tax returns than to an increase in the share of estates given over to bequests. In passing, it is worth mentioning that the 300 per cent increase in total estates between 1950 and 1965 is due to a combination of four factors: there was a 26 per cent increase in the number of deaths, a 179 per cent increase in the proportion of deaths requiring the preparation of an estate tax return, a 247 per cent increase in the number of estate tax returns filed, and a 14 per cent increase in the size of the average estate. In view of continuing economic growth, of further aging of the population, and of the structure of estate taxation, these same factors seem likely to continue to cause further disproportionate increases in total estates and philanthropic bequests in the future.

In contrast to the stability of giving by individuals as a share of the resources available to them, the share of resources available to foundations and corporations represented by their total contributions, gifts, and grants has shown a marked increase. For both donor groups the appropriate ratios doubled in the years after 1950.

In the case of foundations (excluding corporate foundations), the appropriate definition of resources available is not easy to establish, and the information which can be assembled is not complete. Since most foundation funds are derived from various endowment investments, it is appropriate to compare the total with aggregate property income in the United States.

The growth of property income between 1950 and 1968 amounted to almost 260 per cent; the growth of foundation philanthropy in this period amounted to roughly 760 per cent. Clearly the growth of income is not sufficient to explain all the growth of foundation philanthropy. The share of total property income represented by foundation philanthropy rose from 1.09 per cent to 2.64 per cent; this proportion doubled between 1950 and 1960 and has since continued to increase although at a slower pace. What this means is simply that the foundation has been used increasingly as a vehicle for channeling funds for philanthropy from individuals to the ultimate recipients. This is borne out in the rise of the number of foundations and the growth of foundation grants as a component of total philanthropy.

In the case of business corporations, the picture is similar to that for foundations. Total corporate contributions to philanthropic activities increased from $217 million in 1950 to $950 million in 1968, a rise of 338 per cent. Net income before taxes, on the other hand, rose from $37.7 billion in 1950 to $87.9 billion in 1968, an increase of only 133 per cent. Clearly the growth of corporate income is not adequate to explain the growth of corporate philanthropy. There was a parallel increase in the share of corporate income allocated to philanthropic purposes.

This increase in the share of income which corporations are willing to put to philanthropic uses is an important development. It reflects a significant departure of corporate policy from previous positions of long standing. Among the factors responsible for this shift are a general change in attitude toward social responsibility on the part of corporate management, a clarification of both the common law and the statutory provisions regarding the power of corporations to make donations for philanthropic purposes, and a growing belief that the long-term self-interest of the corporation and its stockholders would be enhanced by certain kinds of philanthropic pursuits.

While both corporations and foundations, as donor groups, have in fact increased the shares of their resources that they are willing to devote to philanthropy, the two groups combined represent such a small fraction of total philanthropy that these changes have not yet had an appreciable impact on the ratio of total philanthropy to national income beyond the 1950-1955 increase. The stability of individual giving continues to dominate the national picture.

Given the rise in total philanthropic giving and the changes in its distribution by source, the growth of voluntary support of higher education reflects the changes in the proportions of total giving that the various donor groups are willing to allocate to higher education as opposed to other areas of philanthropy. The historical record of voluntary support as a percentage of total philanthropy is not precise, but the available evidence makes it clear that this percentage has increased substantially for all groups of donors. In rough terms, the share of institutions of higher education in the philanthropic dollar rose from about 6 per cent in 1950 to about 11 per cent in 1964, and it has stabilized around 11 per cent in the past four or five years.

In summary, the factors which affect the size of voluntary support have all tended to cause an increase in the flow of private gifts and grants to higher education. The growth of resources has been most important in explaining the growth of total philanthropy by individuals. Although this factor has been important also for foundations and corporations, it has been less important than the increase in the share of their resources that these groups allocate to philanthropy. And for individuals and corporations, higher education has succeeded in attracting a rising fraction of the philanthropic dollar. In no case during the period 1950 to 1968 have any of these factors operated negatively for any of the donor groups.

Future Trends

The level of total voluntary support of higher education in 1980-1981 is projected in Dr. Bowen's paper at $2.7 billion, which is roughly 7 per cent of the $39 billion of requirements projected for operating and capital purposes in that year. Both of these figures are expressed in 1968-1969 prices; the actual figures are virtually certain to be higher as a result of continuing inflation. If prices should rise as much in the twelve years ending in 1980-1981 as they did in fact rise in the twelve years ended in 1968-1969, then both figures would need to be increased by 29 per cent to be expressed in then current prices. Thus, total requirements for higher education would be $50 billion, and voluntary support would be $3.5 billion in 1980-1981. In the context of past experience and probable developments, how likely is it that this much support will be realized?

The answer necessarily involves some speculation, but the history and other dimensions of voluntary support provide useful guidelines for narrowing the range of speculation to a degree which is acceptable for most purposes. There is, first of all, the probability that voluntary support will grow because the economy will grow and because educational support, along with other kinds of philanthropy, grows with the national income.

Dr. Bowen's projection for the GNP is based on an assumed rate of growth of 4 per cent per year in real terms. If the national income should grow at the same rate, and if 29 per cent is added for inflation, then the $714 billion of 1968 will become $1,475 billion in 1980. Assuming that the relationship between national income and total philanthropy remains at the 1968 level of 2.23 per cent, then $33 billion will be given for all philanthropic purposes in 1980. If higher education should continue to receive about 11 per cent of total philanthropy, then total voluntary support in 1980 would amount to $3.6 billion—roughly the same as Dr. Bowen's projection.

It is important to note that this results from a very reasonable set of assumptions: that national income will grow at 4 per cent per year on the average, in real terms, that inflation will continue in the future at the same rate as in the past, and that no changes occur in the total philanthropy/national income ratio or in the voluntary support/total philanthropy ratio. Other things being equal, the voluntary support of higher education will grow to $3.5 billion or $3.6 billion simply as a result of the income effect.

Other things, however, will almost certainly not be equal. Developments of the past in regard to philanthropy generally, and in regard to giving to colleges and universities in particular, indicate clearly that changes are likely to occur in the philanthropic share of national income and in the higher educational share of total philanthropy. Both ratios have been higher than their levels of 1967-1968, and both ratios have tended to rise with the passage of time. The prospects are that they will increase in the 1970s.

For the business community there should be some modest increase above the levels of the sixties, if only because a relatively small fraction of the corporate entities have accounted for a disproportionate share of past business giving. As more and more firms reach a significant size there will be a larger fraction of all companies giving to philanthropic purposes at commensurate rates. This upward movement along the corporate income scale has undoubtedly been one of the influences behind the past growth of the ratio of business contributions to business income, and there are good prospects for some continuation of this phenomenon over a future span as long as ten years.

Foundation patterns in the seventies will change appreciably from the recent past, although the precise character of the change may not be apparent for four or five years. The Tax Reform Act of 1969 includes a large number of provisions which will affect the attractiveness of the private foundation as a philanthropic vehicle for wealthy individuals. It circumscribes the operations of existing foundations through an intricate set of new rules, some of which will affect the potential flow of funds for philanthropic purposes. And it raises many uncertainties about the division of foundation resources between external grants and self-financed projects. Although the net effect on philanthropy is not completely clear, it seems highly unlikely that there will be any reduction of the ratio between foundation philanthropy and foundation resources. Indeed, there may well be some further slight increase due to the payout requirements spelled out in the act.

Finally, there is a strong probability that the overall contributions-to-income ratio for individuals will return to the higher levels of the early sixties and then rise even further. The modest growth in this ratio since 1950 is due in part to an upward movement of income per capita which increases the proportion of individuals at various higher income levels. As individual incomes rise, there are two factors which tend to increase contributions faster than income. The first is simply the fact that the individual has increasingly more discretionary power over the disposition of his income as his income rises. This is particularly true for income levels above $20,000-$25,000 a year. Secondly, the progressive structure of personal income tax rates and the deductibility of contributions from taxable income reduces the net cost of giving at the margin, and this reduction increases sharply at higher income levels. Hence, some further rise of the ratio of individual philanthropy to personal income should be expected as a result of future growth of per capita income.

Historically, the rise of the overall contribution/income ratio for individuals is probably due also to the success of various philanthropic recipients in appealing to the generosity of individual givers. Some of this success is due to "moral progress," to higher standards of social welfare, and to greater impulses toward humanitarian action. Some of it may also be due to an extension of the concept of self-interest to include elements of the well-being of the less fortunate and aspects of public health and education and other matters external to the individual. But a part of this success is almost certainly due to improvements in the techniques of fund-raising and to increases in the skill with which these techniques are applied. Although new techniques of fund-raising and further improvements in old ones may encounter diminishing returns, there is no reason to believe that recipient organizations and institutions will not achieve some additional success in persuading individuals to expand their levels of support.

There are, then, good reasons for expecting that total philanthropy will rise not only with the growth in national income but also because of some gain in the share of national income which will be allocated to private philanthropic purposes.

Assuming that total philanthropic giving does rise rapidly during the seventies, what can be said about the share that would flow into the voluntary support of higher education in 1980? As was noted earlier, the share of higher education in total private philanthropy increased from about 6 per cent in 1950 to about 11 per cent in the period since 1964. And virtually all of this relative gain was shown to stem from disproportionate increases in educational support (versus all other causes) in the giving patterns of individuals and business corporations; foundation patterns show volatility, but no trend. Objectively, it is possible to find important influences which will operate favorably for higher education in all three donor areas during the seventies.

For individuals, the principal factor is education itself. The appeal of higher education for philanthropic support is basically rational, not emotional. It involves a somewhat advanced degree of sophistication to understand fully the nature and magnitude of the benefits of voluntary support of education. Consequently, further increases in the levels of educational attainment of the older age groups in the population, which contain most of the potential individual donors, will indirectly raise the relative attractiveness of giving to higher education as compared to all other causes.

This factor will be reinforced by a growth of college alumni, both in absolute numbers and as a proportion of the working population. In the past twelve years, alumni support has amounted to about half of all voluntary support from individuals, and it has been the fastest growing and most stable source of educational contributions. Given the continuing upsurge of college enrollment, which must result in a disproportionate increase in the number of alumni, and at least a constant proportion of alumni providing support, it follows that the number of alumni donors is certain to increase in the seventies. Given also the past record of growth of dollar support from alumni, the close ties between college alumni and the institutions of higher education, and the element of self-interest, it would seem likely that the share of higher education in the total philanthropy of individuals will continue to increase during the years ahead.

The appeal of higher education in the context of total corporate contributions has increased very considerably since 1950. Much of this reaction has undoubtedly been pragmatic in character. Business has experienced chronic shortages in the supply of technical, scientific, and administrative talent—in fact, of qualified labor generally. The growth of business support of colleges and universities has in part been merely an effort by the individual firm to ensure that it would have competitive access to college graduates in their programs of recruitment. In part, also, such support has been a concomitant of the "knowledge explosion," and for many industries the productivity of funds allocated to research has been much higher for university-sponsored programs than for "in-house" efforts. The trends in both of these areas have been for more rather than less business aid to education, and more to such an extent that higher education has received a growing share of the contributions dollar from the corporate comunity.

In addition, the institutions of higher education have succeeded in obtaining a growing share of corporation philanthropy not only as a result of growing professionalism and skill in the academic development activity, but also because of growing professionalism and orderly administration on the part of the corporate contributions function. One significant change in the organization of corporation philanthropy since World War II is the gradual shift, still in progress, from passive to active program administration. Business firms now seek out, with full-time personnel and on an ever-increasing scale, new opportunities for the effective application of their contributions dollars in all areas of philanthropy. And in a competitive sense, the institutions of higher education have a slight advantage over other recipients. They can provide the corporate contributor not with opportunities to make charitable donations to worthy causes, but with opportunities to make intangible investments of a philanthropic character which yield demonstrable long-run rates of return to the donors comparable to those from tangible investments of a conventional, profit-oriented character. The preference for the latter type of corporate giving is obvious, and it helps to explain the uptrend in the higher-education/total-philanthropy ratio for the corporate community.

Finally there is the question of foundations and the share of their grants going to higher education. The most likely prospect here is for a continuation of the past volatility. As with corporations, the appeal of higher education in the grants programs of foundations may well grow stronger in the next decade. However, foundation giving is generally less conventional than corporate and individual philanthropy, and it seems probable that innovative and experimental projects will continue to command an important share of foundation interest, perhaps even a growing share. Certainly the competition for foundation funds among the principal classes of recipients will not diminish. And the inherent "lumpiness" of large foundation grants as seed money for new ideas suggests that the educational percentage of all foundation philanthropy will continue to vary significantly.

On balance, therefore, the outlook is favorable for some further increase in the share of higher education in total philanthropy. It is significant that the probability of this taking place is highest for individuals, for this carries the greatest weight in the determination of the overall result. Although the extent of this prospective improvement is uncertain, one may hazard a guess that the ratio will increase to between 13 per cent and 14 per cent of total philanthropy. And if total giving should in fact reach a level of $37 billion or more by 1980, then the voluntary support of higher education would then amount to approximately $5 billion. This is $1.5 billion higher than Dr. Bowen's rough projection for 1980.

If achieved, this flow of voluntary support to the institutions of higher learning will provide an essential underpinning to the financial requirements of colleges and universities. It would constitute roughly 10 per cent of the income likely to be needed in 1980-1981, a proportion higher than achieved in the sixties but comparable to that prevailing in other past periods. More importantly, it would provide the basis for a less significant increase of involuntary support, i.e., governmental appropriations from tax sources. The value of such a potential development should be articulated, for it bears on the quality of future social developments for the entire country.

Problems as Opportunities

EDGAR F. KAISER

Although the nation has accomplished much in the past ten years, it has fallen short of its full potential. Some of its problems have been intensified not only by lack of sufficient effort, but also by the increasing velocity of the winds of change. Which of these problems demand a high priority on the agenda for the 1970s? A consideration of this question is the sound way to examine the nation's choices in higher education, for problems are only "opportunities in work clothes."

William McChesney Martin of the Federal Reserve Board once admonished an audience on the use of statistics. He said: "Statistics should be used like a drunk uses a lamp post—for support and not illumination." A few statistics can be cited, then, not for illumination, but in support of some basic conclusions about the American system of society.

At the start of the 1960s, the stated goal of primary domestic importance was maintaining a steady prosperity while spurring a faster pace of economic growth. About that same time, leaders in business, education, and government began to discuss publicly the imperfections of society and of the system, the tragedies of discrimination, poverty and hunger here at home, the problems of unemployment, of decaying cities, of environmental pollution, and rising discontent with the *quality* of the American way of life.

While openly recognizing and expressing mounting concern about such problems and inequities, the nation seemed to believe that economic growth, in and of itself, would somehow provide the solutions. It was hoped that a faster rise in the gross national product would sweep these problems away in a floodtide of abundance.

In the past ten years, the GNP has increased by nearly 50 per cent. Spendable income for the average American has increased by nearly a third, even after adjustments for inflation and rising taxes. By those two measurements, one can look back on success in the 1960s, despite the tightening pinch of inflation. By still another measurement, the number of students enrolled in college, the 1960s again were clearly years of increasing abundance and progress. College enrollment in that decade more than doubled, from three million to six million students. Anyone sending a youngster through college can hardly argue this figure is not indicative of an affluent society. It is interesting to note that this increase of three million students equals the *total* growth in college enrollment during the preceding three hundred years, from the founding of Harvard in 1658 to the freshman classes of 1959.

As for the business sector during the past ten years, five hundred of the largest industrial firms set new records in sales, earnings, and total employment. In 1969, these firms employed sixty-nine out of every one hundred American wage earners, a record figure in American economic history. This rising tide in abundance won a major battle in the continuing war on poverty. In the 1960s some 14 million Americans rescued themselves from deprivation and raised their family incomes above the federal poverty level. There is no doubt about the meaning of these statistics. The American system, without question, is unequalled in mankind's history in terms of delivering more material goods, more opportunity, and more personal freedom to the vast majority of its participants. The system not only works, it excells.

Yet, despite these major strides toward greater abundance, some discouraging statistics remain and are seized upon by those who would shatter the system with social and economic revolution without either constructive or practical alternatives. In this time of unequalled general prosperity, there is no denying that 26 million Americans, thirteen in every one hundred, still remain entrapped in the clutches of poverty. Although it is estimated that 70 per cent of these poor families are white, the individual economic penalties of racial and ethnic discrimination remain undeniably real and apparent in American society today. In housing, for example, one in every four minority families is unable to afford decent shelter, compared to one in every twelve among the white majority.

If you are a member of a black minority, chances are that you are paying three times more for shelter than your white economic counterparts, regardless of your income. Chances are, too, that you are three times more likely to be living in poverty, twice more likely to be out of work, and your children are three times more likely to die in birth or infancy for lack of adequate medical care. This situation leads to frustration and disillusion at best, and, at worst, to despair or violent protest.

The deficiencies in the system and the penalities of poverty and discrimination are reflected in education as well. Despite a doubling in both student enrollment and institutional spending, the likelihood of children from middle- and upper-income families completing college is three times more probable than the chances of children from families below the median of society's income groupings. Among the black minority, however, only half as many youngsters go on to college as do their counterparts in the white majority. And half of today's black students are attending predominantly black colleges. It is generally agreed among educators that most of these colleges, not necessarily through any fault of their own, are lagging behind the progressive mainstream of American higher education.

Meanwhile, from the scientific community, the voices of dedicated ecologists are predicting that if present trends continue unchecked, the nation will some day have polluted its own environment beyond the point of human survival. In admitted and deliberate exaggeration, some scientists envision a future, not distant, when the inland lakes will be congealed into useless masses of jelly, too thick for floating a boat but still too thin to walk on.

Without any exaggeration whatsoever, they estimate the cost to the nation from air pollution alone is now $12 billion a year in damage to crops, livestock, and property. This is not to mention the most serious damage of all, the harmful effects of pollutants on today's population and on the genetics of the future.

During the affluent 1960s it became clear that an uninterrupted tide of general prosperity alone cannot provide a total cure for the nation's domestic problems. The poor and the racial minorities are still reaching out for the concentrated, coordinated, well-planned programs which will offer them not a hand-out, but a hand-up, to help them help themselves into the mainstream of American life. Tragically, for themselves as well as for society itself, some have lost faith in the system and attack it with scathing rhetoric and sometimes violent assaults.

Among people generally, the affluence of the 1960s seems, ironically, to have kindled an intensifying spark of discontent. People seem to be asking themselves in this rapid surge of productivity, in this age of breathtaking technological achievements, whether they may be missing something in life. They seem to be thinking that perhaps the nation has gone too far, sacrificing taste and style and individual choice in the interest of economy and efficiency. They recognize that the age of instant worldwide communications, coupled with incredible technological capabilities like landing men on the moon, necessitates quick, decisive commitments. They realize that all of these factors necessarily require more centralization of decision-making powers. Yet they seem to be asking themselves: What happens to individual options? How can one individual speak his mind in a voice that is heard? If one writes to his congressman or his state representative, by the time the postal system delivers his letter three or four days later, the issue before the House is closed. How can one make his opinion felt and effect constructive change?

The nation's children, potentially its greatest asset, know that they will inherit the system. Their dominant question is and will be whether they really want it, whether the old canons of business and of other institutions in the system really make sense, not only in terms of material output, but, equally important, also in terms of human values. Some have already decided against the system and express their negativism in strident shouts for revolution and in angry acts of violence against the so-called establishment that they publicly deplore. Others are still questioning, still seeking. They are looking to leaders of the system for help in deciding their answer. The youngsters who are still waiting and watching, still willing to work in the system toward a goal of constructive change, constitute the overwhelming majority.

Often their elders are quick to overreact, too hasty to taint and dismiss all youth of today because of the intolerable destruction and wanton antisocial behavior of the extremist minority. Violence always makes headlines, which too easily can warp perspectives and cause people to react in a precipitous way. If one reacts out of anger, abandoning wisdom, one may win political popularity today. But the result will be the further alienation of the peaceful but questioning majority of American youth.

What are the facts on campus unrest? In the thirteen years of the so-called Movement—the student rebellions—outbreaks of violence have claimed some 220 lives and inflicted some $162 million in damage to public and private property. The figures, to be sure, are tragic and shocking. Yet, in just thirty-six typical hours on the nation's streets and highways, careless drivers kill the same number of lives. And traffic accidents at the current rate inflict just about an equal loss in damage to property every five days. Of course, these figures on student violence are cause for grave concern. And certainly the perpetrators must pay penalities as determined by due process within the system of laws, on and off the campus, that they so flagrantly and deliberately violate. These statistics are cited not to condone or to apologize for destructive youth, but only in an attempt to place the campus violence in some kind of rational perspective.

So far, in the clashes between youth and the American system, the colleges and their administrations have been almost the sole front-line targets. Institutions of higher education have taken the brunt of not only the violent protests from the militant minority, but also the nonviolent demands for change and the penetrating questioning by the majority of youth. Ironically, with a national mood that seems to recognize the necessity for constructive change, what many educators say they are most concerned about, in looking ahead, is a wave of anti-intellectualism in American life.

The concerns of our educators are not without foundation. Too often, society is quick to criticize the leaders in higher education for their response to these campus troubles. Time and time again bond issues for higher education fail to win voters' approval because of shortsighted reactions to campus unrest and the universities' methods and tactics in responding to the problems.

Colleges and universities, both public and private, which have experienced these confrontations are now finding it more and more difficult to raise the funds required for future growth, not only among their own alumni but from business and government as well. Furthermore, it is no coincidence that two hundred presidencies of colleges and universities are vacant today. Many of these vacancies exist not for lack of qualified educators, but because those who are qualified feel there is a crisis of confidence on the part of those whose support they require in order to do the job on the campus that needs to be done.

When one looks ahead to the challenges of the seventies, the highest priorities are clear. The nation must direct more tangible efforts and more thoroughly planned and coordinated programs, with business, education, and government working together toward eliminating the pockets of poverty. The nation must come to recognize that new levels of social involvement are morally right, in addition to being in its own self-interest.

Secondly, while striving to help the poor help themselves and to continue increasing the "quantity" of life generally, steps must also be taken to concentrate, in full earnestness, on improving the quality of life. In meeting both priorities, better tools are available than ever before. New planning methods—systems analysis, working with or without computers—provide new capabilities for measuring choices and determining their comparative costs and benefits to society. We have the tools and the know-how to form our choices intelligently without delaying the decision-making process, and then, once the choice has been made, to plan a course of action with equal intelligence.

Businessmen are prepared to act in response to the challenges within the framework of the existing system. The principal finding in a recent *Fortune 500* survey concluded "that business has begun to accept responsibility for a surprisingly wide range of public problems without, however, modifying the priority assigned to profits. And business leaders are personally eager to make a contribution to their society over and above the management of their business."

There is reason to believe that the 1970s will mark the real and strong beginnings of a renaissance movement within the American system. Business has shown time and time again that once it understands the problems, once the pressures start building, it can and will respond to almost any challenge. The renaissance movement, however, will require renaissance men and women. Business will need more and more people who can properly be called the change-makers. These are the personnel, irrespective of their day-to-day functions, who act as the sources of change and innovation within the corporate structure. They are the generators of new ideas and attitudes on everything from entering new lines of business, or developing new products, to implementing racial integration or prodding the corporation into a greater sense of its social responsibilities. The change-makers are the ones who generate the forces that keep a corporation from becoming mossy-backed and solidified. They rock the boat.

In any corporation, the number of change-makers is usually small. Yet their drive and persuasion, amplified by business's economic and social power, make them among the most socially significant group within the entire corporate structure. Unfortunately, these change-makers already are in woefully short supply. But even more tragic is the fact that prospects for increasing their number appear to be diminishing.

A recent survey of American college students, the main source for change-makers of the future, showed that only 31 per cent of those questioned were considering a career in business. And among the group, only 12 per cent listed business as their first choice. The clear conclusion is that today's college youth, the children of change, seriously doubt whether business will be where the action is. More conscious of the system's imperfections than any preceding generation and more dedicated to helping achieve constructive change, they are skeptical about the ability and commitment of business to address itself to the nation's social problems and combine quality with quantity in producing goods and services. These are not the turned-off, freaked-out, disaffected minority of students. Neither are they the hard core of angry extremists. To the contrary, they include all kinds of students.

How does one reach these children of change? How does one respond to their questions, once a dialogue has been established? Where does one turn for help in restoring their wavering confidence in the abilities and motivations of American business? The actions of business leaders, of course, will help. They must speak with more candor, and the problems and failures of the economic system must be reviewed as well as its successes. But equally important, the nation's educators must help. One of the most pressing needs in meeting the challenges of the 1970s is a new and closer relationship between business and education.

Institutions of higher learning, both public and private, already have experienced the first waves of shock when youth began rudely awakening them with allegations of their irrelevancy and demands for instant change. Ill-prepared as some of these institutions may have been to respond to the challenge, they learned rapidly. As they listened, they discovered what some students really meant in talking about "nonnegotiable demands," "relevant curriculum," and "meaningful dialogue," and in speaking disparagingly of a "plastic" world around them.

Business leaders, in trying to reach these young Americans, have much to learn from the educators. For too many years, business and education have traveled their separate ways, each cognizant of their mutual dependency, but each somehow holding its silent suspicions of the other.

To be sure, the campus is not totally strange, new turf to business. The university has always been the main hunting ground for its personnel recruiters. Many business leaders serve on college boards of trustees, as loyal alumni, or in evidence of their community concern. Sometimes a leading professor is called on as a management consultant or a knowledgeable mediator in a labor dispute. Key executives from major corporations have been attending and participating in continuing educational programs at leading universities in order to keep pace with new management tools and methods. And, of course, business leaders have always given of their time, and sometimes of their money, when the local university president sought support for a new building or a scholarship fund.

On the college campuses, for lack of frequent and substantive contacts, the ghost of the so-called organization man still haunts the halls of learning. He is the antihero of *The Status Seekers, The Executive Suite,* and *The Man in the Grey Flannel Suit.* His image repells the youth of today. In the corporate corridors, there is a lingering tendency for businessmen to look upon the typical college educator as the ghost of Mr. Chips—gentle, kindly, outstanding in intellectual theory, but somehow not with it. In hindsight, and this may be a surprising discovery when one really stops to ponder it, no other social institutions have more in common than business and education.

Both deliberately provide an environment for developing the creative talents of the individual. Both work to guide those talents in the direction of social or economic good. And both now face the common challenge of persuading young America that working within the system is the most effective way to implement change.

In a society whose institutions are buffeted on all sides for demands for more-rapid change, the necessity for a merger of ideas and purposes between business and education has never been greater. Business and education can be the cutting edges of change. To sharpen blades for the challenges of the 1970s, several inputs are now required in a changing business-university relationship. To combat the growing and disturbing mood of anti-intellectualism, universities need the strong, outspoken, public support and the understanding and confidence of business leaders.

The universities also need financial support in substantially increased levels of corporate giving. In order to enable higher education to serve society to its fullest capabilities in the decade ahead, business must be ready to give, and give until it hurts. Both confidence and financial support are equally essential to maintain the nation's institutions of higher learning as open societies where truth and knowledge may honestly be pursued in freedom from externally imposed political and financial controls.

Giving money alone will not be enough. The time and effort of business leaders are needed in equal full measure. Business needs to understand the problems confronting leaders in education. And then the two groups must join together in working to achieve the solutions. It is not enough to send corporation personnel recruiters and community relations specialists to visit college campuses. This new, innovative partnership between business and education calls for top-management time and attention. In the long view, American higher education has earned the nation's support in both dollars and confidence. Despite all the problems on the campus, the universities have never served American society better than they do right now.

Business needs help from educators in reaching the youth of today. There is no question that the product of higher education, the current college graduates, has never been better qualified intellectually to inherit tomorrow's positions of leadership. Industry needs help and advice from educators in improving the student's perception not only of corporate life, but also of the corporation as an institution both concerned with, and relevant to, the humanistic values of life and as an entity capable of bringing about constructive change.

The challenge is to find the way to motivate youth into channeling their energies toward constructive reform. Their fading confidence in the goals and intents of business must be restored. They must be convinced by the words and deeds of corporation executives that the American system, recognizing all of its imperfections, still holds the greatest hope for producing both the "quantity" and the quality of life and the equality of opportunity that all society rightfully expects of it.

One must also recognize that a similar crisis exists in elementary and secondary education affecting the most influential and formative years of children. Statistics for the 1960s indicate that 30 per cent of American youngsters—three in every ten—are dropping out before receiving a high school diploma. Equally tragic is the fact that among those who do finish high school, only four in five receive an education of average quality. This situation presents a clear challenge.

The problems of primary and secondary education need attention. This applies not only to public schools but private institutions as well. Private schools are free from constraints and legislative controls in experimenting with new curricula and new teaching methods. They can be the proving grounds for sound, new theories and experiences in instruction and learning which then can be transferred to the public school systems. They, too, however, face a financial dilemma in planning for the future and in implementing their innovative plans for change.

Traditionally, they have depended primarily on their alumni for the bulk of their financial needs. But the alumni alone can no longer carry the burden. This is particularly true for those private institutions which already are responding to the challenges and economically integrating their student bodies with scholarship programs for less-privileged pupils. Many, by necessity, are turning to business for financial help. While the thrust of this symposium is higher education and business, one cannot afford to overlook the preparatory stages in the total educational process. The problems in primary and secondary education demand a high priority in business's concern and attention and financial help.

The challenges of the 1970s are upon us already. If left unmet, they will only intensify in their malignancy and remain on the agenda for the 1980s, tragically compounded, eroding the strength of the nation's fiber, and becoming more deeply entrenched in the entire economic and social structure.

We can and will respond to these challenges. Failure is foreign to the lexicon of both the corporation and the campus. There is every reason to believe that the age of American renaissance will supplant the age of doubt and questioning in the 1970s. Business and education, working together in a new and constructive alliance, will be in the front line, the moving forces of this renaissance, in response to the mutual challenges. The future of this nation demands nothing less.

Corporate Support of Higher Education

Money for higher education is available from a limited number of sources, which are broadly categorized as private and public. Private sources include that help which the student is able to give himself, whether it comes from work, loans, scholarships, or family contributions. Institutional earnings also contribute to private support. This ranges from the income that colleges and universities have from such diverse enterprises as the college press and the dining hall. It also includes income from endowments and gifts from alumni, friends, corporations, and charitable organizations. Public sources refer rather broadly to income available from the government, federal, state, and local.

Dr. Howard R. Bowen has set forth in detail how the cost of higher education is on the increase. This means, of course, that there is automatically created a greater need for income for the rising cost of education. As one examines the possibilities of increasing income from the primary sources just noted, one quickly discovers that they are not bright and promising. Some idea of the seriousness of the state of finance for higher education can be obtained by examining the possibilities for revenues from private sources.

Students and their parents are now bearing about 30 per cent of the cost of their education. This is about all they can bear, and yet the cost is steadily rising. A recent survey of the National Association of State Universities and Land Grant Colleges has reported one of the sharpest cost increases in recent years. The association reports that at its 117 member institutions the median cost for tuition and fees for a resident student increased 16.5 per cent over the last year. For nonresidents the median rose 13.6 per cent. This survey was limited to public-supported institutions where tuition and fees are normally lower than at private institutions, but it suggests that similar sharp increases have been experienced at private institutions.

Institutional earnings are mostly in the form of endowment income. Few auxiliary enterprises are income-producing; they are more likely to be income-draining or to operate at the break-even point. Only a favored few of the institutions of higher education have endowments which are capable of producing significant returns. Most college endowments are very modest and administered conservatively.

A committee of the Ford Foundation recently recommended sweeping changes in the management of educational endowments. The major recommendation calls for a shift from the policy of investing the funds in stocks and bonds that promise comparatively sure dividends to a policy that favors common stocks of long-term growth potential. By following this suggestion, the committee feels that the total return will be greater, providing more operating funds and increasing growth potential of the investment. An earlier report of the Ford Foundation had challenged the notion that capital gains from endowment funds could not be spent because they are a part of the principal rather than income.

If colleges and universities choose to heed the suggestions of the foundation, there will probably be some modest increases. Yet, it must be remembered that endowments account for only 3.4 per cent of the private source of income. An increase will be helpful, but it is hardly likely that the increase will exceed a small amount. Gifts and grants from alumni and friends should be an area for extensive development. Most colleges and universities are aware of the need to encourage giving among their alumni and friends, but recent events have tended to discourage this potential source.

The recent federal tax reform bill provides for a revision of the federal income tax, designed to eliminate special privilege and to correct inequities; but it may have negative effects on education through regulation of foundation activities. At a time when private schools, colleges, and universities are fighting desperately to survive as centers of learning, any new limitations placed on gifts to these institutions will prove crucial and will increase their dependence on state and federal funds. The tax laws of the past encouraged phil-anthropic giving, but the new legislation will eliminate major in-centives to giving by placing restrictions on appreciation in the value of securities. Foundation giving has been of vital importance to education, but, sadly, there are indications of changes which point to the end of this support.

As for public support of education, there are already indications of serious budgetary limitations on the state and local level. If there is to be more public support, it will have to come from the federal government, and there are serious questions as to the advisability of extending federal support beyond an optimum level. The Carnegie Commission's report, "Quality and Equality," contained a great deal of useful information; but its major recommendation was that the fifty-fifty division of the cost of education between the public and private sectors should be maintained. The commission report unequivo-cally states that government participation in the cost of higher edu-cation should not exceed 50 per cent.

These, then, are the possibilities for and the limitations upon increased financial aid for education, supporting the contention of Dr. Bowen, who, in an address delivered at the National Higher Education Association in the spring of 1969 in Chicago, said: "The political climate in which education is operating today is less favor-able than it was a decade ago. Today, higher education presents an appearance of success, even affluence. . . . The increased visibility and influence brought it under close political scrutiny. Public officials, worried about budgets, are searching for ways to retard the rapid escalation of all education costs."

The changed political climate and the prospects for even greater alterations in the ability of education to get financial support from the usual sources are serious for higher education, and serious for the nation. Changes in the tax structure will undoubtedly influence the giving habits of the public. All schools depend on the big gift, no matter how many small gifts they get. Capital campaigns especial-ly depend on the big gift, and these campaigns will be particularly hurt by the proposed tax bill.

The changes and the challenges to sources of public and private support will affect all of education, but it will have a particularly deleterious effect on the less-prestigious schools. The large, well-known colleges and universities are usually well organized and able to maintain professional staffs for development and promotion which are highly paid and active. Such colleges usually have a wider base for support because of the large number and affluence of their graduates, the quality of their faculty, and the abundance of their research. The big financial crunch will fall on the smaller, less-known institutions which have fewer contacts, fewer friends, little research, and already rely heavily on government support and a greater percentage of student cost. The limitations just cited are likely to place the cost of education out of reach of those who are not wealthy, and to deny educational opportunities to numerous young people. These prospects are not good for America, and they are not good for the enlightened self-interest of the business community. As public and other private sources are obviously limited in their abilities to meet the new needs of education, it becomes necessary for the business community to fill the void.

Business leaders are quick to ask where savings may be effected and where the system can be changed to eliminate some of the daily costs. This is a legitimate question, and educational institutions must be able to defend their methods of operation. This matter of academic administration is a greatly neglected area, and even though degree programs are offered in higher education, it is unlikely that there is an adequate training program for the kind of administration demanded today any more than there is an adequate educational program for chief executives of corporations.

Colleges and universities can do a great deal to assure wise and prudent administration. Many colleges have cut costs by limiting degree programs, cutting duplicate courses, and by more efficient methods of management. Business should help more colleges wisely shepherd their resources. The computer age has greatly affected higher education administration, and the new technology demands that administrative organization keep apace. Business organizations can help. Colleges and universities must respond.

Industry must also help in the more tangible aspects of support to higher education. Of all voluntary support to higher education, 85 per cent comes from individuals and charitable organizations. Given the political mood of Congress and the present political climate, there is no doubt that there will be an adverse effect on contributions to education from individuals and foundations. The necessity of the corporate gift becomes even more urgent.

Corporate generosity becomes more urgent when one considers that there is a distinct difference between what corporations regard as support to education and what institutions of higher education term support. Corporations are inclined to include a variety of special grants and projects among their contributions to education—such items as scholarships and fellowships, support to secondary education and "dropout" programs, tuition refund and scholarship plans, support of educational television, support of special research, and contributions to particular professions. As important as these items are, they do not represent the visceral factors of higher education where expanded funds for physical plant and faculty salaries are desperately needed.

Corporations may ask, Why support education? When one is faced with directors, stockholders, and employees; directed by regulations and standards; and concerned with unions and security analysts, one is called on to justify every action. In his Chicago speech, Dr. Bowen said: "Perhaps more important than the political climate is the increasing competition of new claimants for public and philanthropic dollars." He listed some of those claimants as poverty programs, urban renewal, housing, health care, space exploration, and economic development of emerging nations. If corporations gave to every worthwhile cause, they would exhaust the source of their gifts.

Some feel that universities will be recipients of funds as they become involved in some of the social and economic problems which need the research techniques and consultative expertise to be found on the campus. It is true that many universities will be involved in many of the new and expanding programs, and will share moneys apportioned for research, and the competition for funds will probably intensify in this area.

How, then, does one justify increased investments in higher education? First, any investment in higher education is an investment in the self-interest of the corporations. The colleges and universities of the nation are producing the young men and women who will fill corporate vacancies. Obviously, an investment in young people assures business a supply of chemists, engineers, statisticians, business managers, marketing experts, and technicians. Second, businessmen who are committed as the protectors and defenders of the American system of economics know that an educated people will help protect and defend the free system of economic enterprise which they value.

As one considers some of the colleges, the question may be asked whether they are worth supporting. It appears that the bearded and sandaled student has little interest in the free enterprise system or in any other system. It is well, however, to bear in mind that those who are most visible and the loudest represent only a very small per cent of the total university population, and that even the most bearded and sandaled antihero has a way of growing up and accepting responsibility. Not many years ago, there was a "lost" generation followed by a "beat" generation. The lost became found, and the beat became rejuvenated. There is hope even for the hairy and shoeless.

Again, education needs support because the nation profits from the fruit of basic research and from the knowledge explosion. It is only self-interest to support scientific research which will make a tremendous impact upon business operations in products, methods, or in some other way.

Figures can get to be confusing. However, to demonstrate the breadth and intensity of the problem, a few facts will perhaps help. The best estimate of corporate giving, of what corporations are doing now, is the 1968 figure of $340 million. About 70 per cent of this figure constituted a sharing of the business community in the needs of the colleges and universities. Thirty per cent of this sum went for scholarships, student aid, tuition grants, and educational activities, many of which may not be regarded as contributions but as normal business expenses. For the next decade, it is essential that the corporate community increase its support to general education, and that a share be designated for colleges and universities. Between 1958 and 1968, corporate support grew 10 per cent each year. It is essential that this level of contribution be maintained, at least for the next ten years. Even though the share of college and university expenditures declined during the 1960s, college expenses will not accelerate as greatly in the years to come, and the corporate share of the increase for the twenty-year period would still be a respectable 10 per cent. If corporate support continues to grow at the 10 per cent rate, by 1980 corporations should be contributing $1 billion.

The power and value of education needs no defense. It should be foremost in corporate deliberations, not only because of what it means to the country's corporations, but because of what it means to the corporations' country.

The Corporation and the Community

JAMES F. OATES, JR.

The troubles of the cities are so vast and pervasive that the nation's colleges and universities must seek additional financial support, much of it from corporate business, in order to play their part in alleviating the tragic human conditions of poverty, disease, unemployment, and despair. There is thus a heavy and mounting burden on the corporate contributions' dollar.

It is clear that the ties between businessmen and educators which have been mutually advantageous through the years must be maintained and developed. There exist no sharp lines separating their fundamental motivations, purposes, and moral objectives. Their goals for full and free expression and development of all men and women are much the same—and, indeed, are shared by Americans generally. Thus the corporate viewpoint, if it exists separately at all, will not be suprisingly different from others.

On the other hand, business corporations are essentially economic institutions. While their operations are economic, their consequences are inevitably social. The view that the corporation has no proper interest in the public welfare is no longer true, if it ever was. But this does not mean that the corporation should not seek to make optimum, long-term profits. Of course it should.

One must look beyond this oversimplified concept, however, and view profit in three contexts—of time (long-term profitability rather than short-term gain), of size (the larger a business becomes the more it is asked to respond to the problems of society and to demonstrate its social content), and, most important, of the further contributions that business can make (as the corporation matures and a deeper understanding of its role in society evolves, it can be plainly seen that its success is directly related to the health of the larger society). Consequently, it is compelled to contribute to the welfare of the community by economic as well as moral considerations.

The nature and scope of the urban problem call for the best efforts, at all levels, of private business and higher education as well as of governmental authorities. Some examples may help to illustrate this statement.

For two years now, the nation's leading life insurance companies have been diverting from their normal stream of investments hundreds of millions of dollars for investment in city core areas throughout the country as part of a historic $2-billion pledge to the nation. The latest report shows that over $1 billion has been committed so far, all aimed at improving housing conditions and financing job-creating enterprises where they are needed most. This money, thus far, is building nearly 80,000 housing units and has created or retained nearly 40,000 jobs. The Equitable Life Assurance Society of the U.S. has pledged some $170 million to this program, and already has committed or disbursed well over $111 million of this amount. What has been accomplished in this program so far will perhaps suggest how vital and meaningful such investments can be and why the need is so great for more businesses to respond with more action.

In Harlem, for example, these investments have helped to create a unique and promising corporate endeavor. Over $1.5 million has been supplied to purchase, enlarge, and remodel a Woolworth Department Store. The important point is that the store will employ 130 additional persons from the Harlem community, and will be owned by the residents of the community and leased to Woolworth.

In Memphis, Tennessee, aid was given to finance the Freedom Shopping Center, consisting of twelve stores owned by and leased to black entrepreneurs. In this venture Equitable acquired a first mortgage of $275,000; the Small Business Administration supplied a second mortgage of $500,000; and black and white investors supplied over $100,000 of venture capital by selling stock to the people in the community at five dollars a share.

In Fresno, California, a medical building is being financed to provide offices and clinical facilities for black doctors, and in

Washington, D.C., mortgage money was provided for the National Health Center nursing home located in and serving the citizens of the so-called ghetto section.

In similar fashion, Equitable has invested amounts ranging from $750,000 to $3.8 million in other localities throughout the country. In the private-housing field—one-to-four family homes—Equitable is making it possible for about 8,500 families in cities across the country to purchase or refinance their homes. The money is being funnelled through local mortgage brokers and a special effort is made to secure working arrangements with mortgage firms owned or managed by blacks. Equitable loans carry an interest rate as much as 1 per cent below market. The terms are up to thirty years, and the amount of the loan is up to 97 per cent of the purchase price. These are all beneficial and not usual or competitive provisions.

In another program of the sort that many corporations have introduced, Equitable made substantial deposits early this year in banks owned and operated by the minorities. This program has been successful in placing such deposits in seventeen banks in fifteen of the cities where the company has headquarters offices.

Equitable officers have also been working hard along with many others to change the company's internal hiring policies. As late as 1960, there were few salaried employees at Equitable from minority groups. Some 15 per cent of these employees are now from minority groups. In the New York home office, the figure is about 20 per cent, and certain to rise. Of high school graduates currently being hired in New York City, 60 per cent are blacks and Puerto Ricans. Every Equitable office throughout the country, including the South, is integrated.

At present some 450 agents out of a sales force of more than 7,600 are from minority groups. There are 48 minority district managers out of 871 and 8 minority agency managers out of 161. These agency managers are men with highest-level executive responsibilities in the field, and each has from twenty to one hundred people reporting to him.

In addition, the home office in New York City is now in its sixth year of a pioneering program for training high school dropouts, largely blacks, for jobs. The program is not a complete success, but there have been substantial accomplishments that make it well worth the effort. A job is the badge of belonging, of membership in the larger society. A paycheck is a passport to self-respect and self-sufficiency. Jobs are a must and business leaders have to work hard in this area if unemployment is to be reduced.

While Equitable would have liked to hire 800 high school youngsters this year, intensive recruiting efforts resulted in the employment of only 550. In efforts to recruit trainable employees, it was recognized that the company had a responsibility to work cooperatively with the schools at the lower levels of the system. In a frankly experimental program, Equitable "adopted" a junior high school in the Bronx last fall, and a program of two-way visits between students and the company's employees is now in full swing. The value of this kind of program is not measurable in one year, or perhaps ever.

In another school-related project, Equitable together with other New York City companies sponsored one-day seminars designed to carry on a dialogue between young Equitable men and women and seventh-and eighth-grade students. Equitable employees participate as "living witnesses" to inform students of opportunities in business and to motivate them to finish high school as a means of preparing for available jobs. There are several other school-related programs in which the company is actively involved.

Equitable's basic approach is to hire minorities at every level of the organization. What a business organization can do, and must do, is open doors so that blacks can enter the regular channels for promotion and advancement, which constitute the pipeline to whatever supervisory or management jobs for which the individual can qualify.

Providing opportunities for minorities at executive levels in a business corporation presents a particularly difficult problem. Universities and colleges can do much at this level in cooperation with business firms. For example, Equitable has recruited personnel at black colleges for a number of years. This year, the company employed a total of 600 college graduates for the home office and the field, and 10 per cent were from minority groups. Where appropriate, the company's college recruits have been enrolled in special development programs to ensure that they will enter the management pipeline on even terms with white college recruits.

In the actuarial area, another problem exists. There are two black actuaries in the United States. One of them works for Equitable. In an endeavor to increase the supply of actuaries, Equitable and five other insurance companies are working with nine black colleges and universities. A summer program in actuarial science for mathematics students from these colleges is now in the planning stage. This program and a continuing program of visiting lectureships in actuarial science will be important steps in opening the actuarial pipeline to blacks.

Joining other companies and five universities—Indiana, Rochester, Southern California, Washington at St. Louis, and Wisconsin —a pioneering program of graduate fellowships in business for blacks has been begun. Students in this program are undertaking the regular Master of Business Administration curriculum. Again the goal is to get more blacks into the pipeline for executive positions.

While recognizing that these programs put heavy demands on the corporate dollar, the obligation that corporations have to support higher education is not reduced in the least. To be sure there is a vicious squeeze on corporate budgets. But Equitable and many other business concerns have tried very hard to increase their rate of giving to higher education in spite of the huge demands for funds to undertake social programs in the nation's cities,

Colleges and universities today are confronted with the need to compete for outstanding faculty, to increase scholarships, to construct buildings, and to provide facilities, as well as to improve the curriculum. Student tuition and other fees at these institutions have increased substantially in recent years, and income from endowment has decreased as a percentage of total annual income. In this situation, corporation's gifts have become even more vital to the future existence of these dynamic and growing institutions which are essential for the welfare of the nation. The partnership between business and higher education must be strengthened. Corporate financial aid must increase and at a faster rate than it has in the past.

This may sound like a herculean task, and it is. But failure is unthinkable. The resources exist within business to assure the continued vitality of the nation's colleges and universities. There is a greater need than ever before to educate more leaders from minority groups. Education is essential to provide a significant segment of future business management, to assure the healthy growth of a rapidly changing society, and to enhance the welfare of all the people.

Technology and Society

A series of interacting, overlapping, or parallel revolutions are now taking place. Two of these are in energy and communications, and each contains profound implications for the psychic, philosophical, and political revolutions underway.

As a result of man's ability to harness and use the energy in such sources as hydroelectric power and fossil fuels, the average amount of power available to each person in the world today is only about 100 watts—weighted quite disproportionately in favor of the industrialized nations, of course. But the availability of energy is growing very rapidly, not only in such forms as solar energy, but also in the "established" form of nuclear power, and a moderate increase in available energy per capita will bring about another industrial revolution.

Simultaneously, and coupled with the revolution in energy, is a basic advance in communication. The enormous change in the quantity of information and the new ways to use it are affecting every aspect of life.

It is this dual technological revolution and its impact on society and business which will be considered here. It is perhaps the central question of the times. What students here and abroad are agitating about is essentially this matter of the quality of life, the generation's whole approach to society. The institutions of higher learning, the source of tomorrow's businessmen and scientists and the seed bed of those who will be making public policy in the future, are in ferment and revolt. The causes of youthful discontent go deep, indeed, deeper even than the issue of war and peace.

One may well ask how the minority residents of slums and other terribly deprived segments of society feel about the American dream. Where, after all the civil-rights bills and antipoverty legislation of recent years, does the nation stand with these people? Indeed there is some danger that parts of the country will be burned to the ground and the central cities sacked by irrational, almost purposeless violence of people who are disillusioned by unkept promises and generations plowed under. How, one may ask, can all this be in a time of unprecedented prosperity, a time of the brightest promise man has ever known? How, when the physical revolutions are so marvelous, can there be such national doubt, such international misery?

The words that Charles Dickens in *A Tale of Two Cities* used to describe the end of the eighteenth century might well apply to the United States today: "It was the best of times, it was the worst of times, it was the age of wisdom, it was the age of foolishness, it was the epoch of belief, it was the epoch of incredulity, it was the season of Light, it was the season of Darkness, it was the spring of hope, it was the winter of despair, we had everything before us, we had nothing before us, we were all going direct to Heaven, we were all going direct the other way . . . ."

Nearly everyone, no matter how limited his education or how fuzzy his thinking, has at least a subliminal realization of the enormous contributions that technology through industry has made to the human condition. Nevertheless, it is true that contributions of technology have not been shared by all segments of society, nor has industry fully met its obligations or made full use of the opportunities provided by technological advances. Yet to bring modern technology to bear on social problems is perhaps one of the biggest opportunities of the present century. It will not be easily accomplished, but it is an opportunity that businessmen and technology-oriented companies must explore if only because they are in many ways the father and the creator of the society toward which the nation is so rapidly evolving. Any corporate planner stumbling toward the future with as little purposefulness as modern society sometimes seems to show would be sacked in short order. George Bernard Shaw expressed his own Draconian view of this truth in these words: "Every person who owes his life to civilized society and who has enjoyed since his childhood its very costly protections and advantages should appear at reasonable intervals

before a properly qualified jury to justify his existence. This existence should be summarily and painlessly terminated if he fails to
justify it. . . . Nothing less will make people really responsible
citizens."

Businessmen and scientists have a moral imperative to extend
both the potential and the fruits of technology, not only to the
frontiers of human development but into its backwaters as well.
Technology, particularly in recent times, has theoretically advanced
the human condition, but in a very spottily, uneven way. Its pace
has left whole segments of American society and, in fact, whole
nations and regions further behind the United States in their development than they were even ten or twenty years ago.

This gap is more dangerous to America, both internally and
externally, than any other fact of the times. As Kahn and Wiener
point out in their recent book, *The Year 2000*, "every society today
is consciously committed to economic growth, to raising the standard of living of its people, and therefore to the planning, direction and control of social change."

Most Americans today would agree that technologically strong
companies, above all others, must relate intimately and continually
to social change because they are the prime motive force in its
direction and development, a positive and inescapable locus of power.
Thus the challenge that must be faced is rather obvious. Can
the nation really do what needs to be done in order to create and
maintain the sort of society that will provide the climate that must
exist if a great number of persons have taken refuge in the assumption that technology is blind? What is meant by this question is
that technology serves men to the extent that those who direct it are
interested in improving the human condition. And the corollary
has been that those men in decision-making positions really are
interested in advancing the human condition. Large numbers of
people simply do not believe this is true because those living in
inner cities and among the suffering have derived little benefit from
modern technology and profit-making private enterprise. Even
some of the most articulate and direct beneficiaries of the system,
the disenchanted students and faculty members, doubt the truth of
this assertion. Yet American business has developed both a sense of
social obligation and a sense of power to meet it. Certainly it has
the power, particularly if one accepts the definition offered by Jean-
Jacques Servan-Schreiber in his extraordinary book, *The American*

Challenge: "Neither legions nor raw material nor capital are any longer the signs of instruments of power. And even factories themselves are only external evidence. Force today is the capacity to invent, that is—research; it is the capacity for converting inventions into products, that is—technology. The deposits one must exploit are no longer in the earth or in the vast populations or in machines —but in the mind. More precisely: in the aptitude of man for reflecting and for creating."

Power is, of course, a double-edged sword and it is still true that "uneasy rests the head that wears the crown." People, including academicians, expect more of those who have power, and often fear them as well. If those in private business, espcially in technology-oriented business, are to retain or deserve to retain power, they must above all persuade people by actions, not speeches, that its exercise is not going to be arbitrary but responsible, perceptive, and humane. This clearly puts a great obligation on businessmen. But this additional obligation is inescapable.

How can a corporation which wishes to make an effort to assume such an obligation organize to do so? This undertaking is extraordinarily difficult because the key points are subtle and intangible. It mostly depends on the spirit that exists at the top level in the corporation. Perhaps the experience of the Xerox Corporation will illustrate this thesis.

Perhaps the most universal social activity of most corporations is that of formal philanthropy. All large companies have contributions programs that encompass, in different forms and with varying approaches, a range of useful causes: aid to education, Community Chests or United Funds, research grants, civic and cultural activities, and aid to minorities. Individual companies, of course, have their unique goals in developing these programs. In Xerox, as in many other companies, the decisions on all philanthropic contributions are made by a small senior-management group after a thorough analysis of proposals has been made by the professional staff. The goal is not merely to respond to requests but to develop new ideas. Much more to the point, flexibility must be maintained in the programs. If the pace of society is indeed as quick as it seems to be, then coporations must be ready and willing to respond to new needs immediately and be unafraid of unorthodox and even controversial programs.

During the past year, for example, Xerox made a rather substantial grant to Planned Parenthood for a study that would hopefully lead to better use of its financial and manpower resources. Although birth control is certainly not a subject characterized by tranquil contemplation, it deserves the attention of everyone even though it may bring protests from those who strenuously oppose it and who believe, wrongly, that any contribution represents an endorsement *in toto* of the organization's goals. Yet if the population explosion is not a proper social concern, what is?

Simultaneously, and at a time when Xerox is spending major new resources on ghetto problems, hard-core unemployment, and retraining of minorities, it also undertook a major commitment to the Metropolitan Museum of Art in New York. Its sponsorship of the Metropolitan's first major centennial exhibition (which is also its first major exhibit of contemporary art), represents the kind of balance that all corporations should seek in their giving programs. If, in an age of social crisis, corporations greatly increase their commitment to the problems that are most urgent and most immediate, they must do so without sacrificing or overlooking the cultural values which strengthen and enrich the fabric of society.

Finally, since all businessmen must be interested in the future, Xerox decided to make some funds available in 1969 to the Hudson Institute to further its seminal studies of the future. Although such "think tanks" are usually oriented toward policy research for government, Hudson's projections of the future, framed in terms of socioeconomic developments around the world, are valuable to all institutions. Not only do they make people aware of the various alternatives available for worldwide economic development, but the imagination applied to those alternatives is "mind-expanding" in the best sense of that term. Thus Xerox seeks in its contributions program to add as many dimensions above and beyond traditional areas of concern as it can. The distance between support for a "think tank" and support for a group of young people who bring psychodrama to the streets of Harlem may seem great, yet the claims of each are cogent and meaningful.

But there is a second and, in some ways even more important, element that can be added to a corporation's efforts. It has to do with the application of the energy of the corporation executives. In every large company there are professional skills that must be brought to bear on specific problems that society is facing. Xerox, for example, has one of the finest microfilm capabilities in the world through one of its operating units, University Microfilms, in Ann Arbor. When floods raced through Tuscany several years ago and endangered the whole city of Florence, the Committee to Rescue Italian Art asked for help. Xerox decided that it could be of greatest value by combining dollars with microfilming to preserve permanently historical documents damaged by the floods. In so doing, it guaranteed that at least a portion of history will not be lost to future scholars.

More recently Xerox helped create the opportunity to contribute the skill of management itself. Too often corporations overlook the fact that management, as a human commodity, is invaluable to those who need it and do not have it. Therefore, in conjunction with a minority group in Rochester, New York, it established an inner-city factory for production of metal stampings and transformers. The plant, which will be owned, operated, and staffed by blacks, is guaranteed $500,000 in sales by Xerox over the first two years. In addition, the corporation provides training and technical and management assistance across the board. Should the enterprise prove successful it could be imitated in many places.

One other program should be mentioned. Xerox has always believed that the medium of television is the most powerful force for communication and understanding that man possesses. Since it began television sponsorship over eight years ago, it has consistently tried to bring to the public programming of the highest order. Its purpose has been to stimulate, to question, to examine, and to bring about a broader understanding of today's institutions, opportunities, and problems. At times, as in 1964, when it sponsored a series of less-known activities of the United Nations, the efforts have resulted in controversy. Some sixty thousand letters were received opposing the sponsorship, and later as many praising it. In the summer of 1968 the company sponsored a seven-part series without commericals designed to bring about a more-balanced understanding of black history and black contributions to the United States, and with the same result.

How does one impose order on all this—on contributions to charitable, cultural, and educational activities, the many training and employment programs designed to help minorities, the supervision of inner-city projects, the goals of the television programming, the commitments of manpower to public affairs, and the hundreds of other involvements that sometimes distract from the business of making a profit in the short term? The answer is that organization and structure are secondary to the ability and willingness of the leaders at the top to foster a spirit of social responsibility that penetrates throughout the ranks of an organization. There are many ways to structure a public-affairs function. All can succeed and, incontrovertibly, all can fail, depending on the insight and commitment of the leaders.

If the purpose of structure is to relieve top management of some burdens of its responsibility, then that structure will fail because it will tend to isolate management from realities. If, on the other hand, management uses the structure as a way of multiplying personal effectiveness, then it will succeed and the spirit of commitment will sift down throughout the corporation. Then even the most junior personnel will find, and will be recognized for finding, creative ways to accomplish good. Put simply, the success of responsible corporate action in contributing solutions to public problems is directly proportionate to social commitment of its leadership.

No other segment of society exerts greater impact on society as a whole than business technologists and the businessmen who decide how to use their efforts. No society will long be willing for any group to hold such power unless the members of that group clearly demonstrate their awareness of the potential consequences of that power and their concern with using it to improve the lot of their fellowman.

Corporate strategists like to think, with a good deal of justification, that they are concerned as much with shaping the future environment as with forecasting it. Actually, this goes back to an earlier time when Sears-Roebuck's business was mainly in rural areas of the country. Nobody thought it was odd for the company to help the farmers increase their income so they could buy more from Sears. There was a direct correlation between farm income and that company's profits. The old Standard Oil Company also exploited this tactic and expanded the market for kerosene by making thousands of lamps available to the people of China.

The primary environment of American business is, of course, America. Because it is becoming increasingly an urban society, the environment of American business focuses on the central cities. Yet these cities are becoming uninhabitable in the view of many people—especially those middle- and upper-class whites who have deserted them in droves for the suburbs. This process naturally feeds on itself.

Political pressures and the urgent requirement for public order are forcing the government into doing more in attacking poverty, slum housing, illiteracy, poor health, and the rest of this sorry syndrome. Yet approaches by government at any level are seldom bold or innovative and often seem to perpetuate the problem, perhaps a subconscious way of perpetuating the machinery and the system and the status quo. Businessmen, on the other hand, want to solve any problems that they tackle or at least to make major improvements and prevent relapses.

Corporation interest in these problems goes beyond that of just expanding markets for goods and services, though it might be mentioned that the United States itself offers the greatest growth potential of any underdeveloped nation on the globe. Americans who have gained almost nothing from the private enterprise system or failed to secure the most highly valued prizes of all, self-respect and dignity, are almost bound to feel that they owe nothing to private enterprise and little to government. If businessmen lend their minds, hands, hearts, technology, and other resources to this effort, a lot may be accomplished.

Still another benefit will be greater ease in recruiting, developing, advancing, and retaining the qualified young people that industry must have as leaders for tomorrow. Today's youth are demanding more from life than a chicken in every pot—or its present-day equivalent, a television set in every room. They are insisting on a certain degree of idealism, a commitment to human progress that is active, intimate, and sensitive. They want an opportunity to render real service to their fellowman as well as to make a good living.

Every age in history has thought that its problems were greater than those of any preceding period. Socrates and Plato expressed great anxiety over the decline in public morality and the rebelliousness of youth. Jefferson, Washington, and Lincoln worried over problems that sound contemporary. One need not argue that the problems society faces today tower over those of earlier generations. The present generation, however, has more tools, more accumulated knowledge, more capable managers, and, most important, better technology to cope with its problems than any that has preceded it.

Criteria for Corporate Aid

CHARLES B. MCCOY

The need for continuing support of higher education by private corporations is clear and documented. The dimensions of the financial need are well known, and the legitimacy of corporate support has been established at law and by practice. The self-interest of the business sector is as much at stake as the interest of any other segment of society, public or private. All must help sustain an educational structure with the capacity to grow and innovate, and to that end corporate support should increase in the 1970s with a larger number of companies participating at a higher average level of grants and gifts.

Not to be overlooked, though, are the qualitative questions that should weigh equally with the quantitative problem. If education in the 1970s is going to concern itself more with questions of quality, as it appears to be doing, it follows that supporters of education (foundations, corporations, government, and individuals) should be similarly concerned. Those who have corporate responsibility for aid-to-education programs must examine their criteria, and, if necessary, change them to assure that grants or gifts provide maximum leverage and value for colleges and universities. How one gives makes as much difference as how much is given.

As a prelude to some remarks on that point, a few observations are in order on the quantitative side. College administrators understandably feel a sense of urgency about their present needs. Construction costs are rising at an alarming rate, and inflation has diluted the buying power of the dollars at hand. Costs per student have risen in terms of everything from cafeteria meals to new equipment for the physics laboratory, which represents more sophisticated tools for learning but is invariably more expensive.

To complicate matters, federal support for university research and graduate science programs has reached a plateau, and in some instances is declining. Fund seekers are obliged to redouble their appeals to other sources in the private sector to take up the slack.

Given these pressures, distinctions between quality and quantity may seem faintly academic. It would be understandable if college fund raisers argued that we should skip the niceties and produce the funds in any way possible. They see their problems of finance as endemic and chronic. No one fund drive, however successful, can do much more than meet current needs and erect a corner of the scaffolding for the future. There will be further needs next year and the year after, no doubt in rising amounts. College fund raisers are to be forgiven if they describe themselves as men on a treadmill, trudging steadily to stay in the same place.

The problem is real enough, but it is unfortunate that medical labels have been attached to it. A chronic condition suggests that the patient is sick and likely to remain so. One might almost infer that, if colleges and universities could only pare their budgets drastically, they would be restored to good health. The inference is false and takes one in the wrong direction.

Without denying that some schools are in a truly precarious position and literally fighting for survival, the financial plight of colleges and universities in general is not to be diagnosed as ill health. It is a sign of growth, and growth on a scale that is frequently not appreciated. Cost figures for education have become so large and have been quoted so often that they have a numbing effect.

It may help to draw upon comparisons. As an example, one might cite research expenditures. In 1940 the total federal budget for research and development in the United States was about $74 million. Today, a few of the largest universities individually report research budgets of that order of magnitude, accounted in part to their teaching role and in part to research-and-development contract projects. Even with an adjustment for inflation, it is clear that three or four large universities, taken together, are today operating science and engineering programs equal in dollar scale, if not in number of practitioners, to the federal effort of a single generation ago.

Other indices of change provide equally impressive illustrations. Colleges and universities are undertaking a vastly expanded role in society, in enrollments, in breadth and diversity of curricula, and in services to the public beyond the campus. It is this, more than inflation or any other factor in the current cost squeeze, on which one should focus his attention.

People have changed their level of expectations. They want more from the educational establishment than was demanded in the past, and what they want is inherently expensive. They want so much that at times they become visibly impatient with what seems to be a slow pace, but in historical terms this society has moved rapidly toward a goal that no other has yet reached and no past generation even considered as a feasible objective.

The basic premise for an educational structure was set forth nearly two thousand years ago by a Stoic philosopher, Epictetus, when he said, "Only the educated are free." Epictetus had first-hand experience in matters of freedom and bondage. Born a slave and later freed, he understood that society does not make a man truly free merely by releasing him from chains. There is still the slavery of ignorance and the bondage of the unprivileged. Only within the lifespan of this nation, a fleeting moment in the long history of man, has any large society been wealthy enough to realize that it can eradicate these forms of servitude for all of its citizenry.

As Francis Keppel pointed out, the goal at first was some education universally available. It was not much—a few years of elementary education, as recently as Thomas Jefferson's time—but it was a beginning. More recently came equality, far too slowly, considering the inequalities and elitism that still exist, but nonetheless an extension of the original goal. The expectation then became more education, on the college level, with more equitable access for blacks and others who previously were left on the perimeter of educational opportunity.

Uniformity carries with it the seeds of mediocrity. Accordingly, quality was added as part of the goal—quality education for the many instead of for the few. It is a worthy goal, one that may be attainable within the lifetime of most now living, but not a goal that can be attained cheaply.

This formidable troika—quantity with equity and quality—is so vast in its dimensions that it requires the earnest support of all sectors of society. It is too important an effort for anyone to shirk. What is the role of the private corporation? How much can it do?

It would be realistic to admit that the corporation, of and by itself, can do very little in comparison to the scale of the need. Figures assembled by the Council for Financial Aid to Education show that, as of the 1967-1968 academic year, business corporations provided about 16 per cent of the voluntary support for a survey group of 861 colleges and universities.

For the sake of argument, assume that in the decade ahead contributions from the business sector will grow in relative as well as absolute terms, thus representing a larger percentage of total voluntary support. As a high-end estimate, set corporate support for 1980 at 25 per cent of voluntary giving. This is merely an exercise in arithmetic and not a sober projection; yet even if it were to come true, the total of corporate grants and gifts would represent less than 2 per cent of the present forecast of overall financial needs for colleges and universities in 1980.

One is therefore driven back to the question of quality. Are there ways to enhance the educational value of corporate support? Is it a matter of tossing contributions into the pot and hoping for the best, or are there criteria by which corporate gifts can be given leverage and even unique value?

Most corporations clearly believe that such criteria should be sought and applied. They have avoided for the most part the bread-upon-the-waters approach, in the conviction that bread so scattered becomes nothing but crumbs. They have focused their gifts in selected areas, for a limited number of colleges and universities, according to their own corporate definitions of objectives.

There appears to be no great consistency in the criteria they use, unless it is to be found in a corporate bias toward support of science and engineering. Nor is consistency an end in itself. To the contrary, there is merit in a pluralistic structure in which each organization fashions its own link-pins to education, with the same resulting diversity that is found among individual givers and private foundations.

The major question is whether this diversity, based on the needs and interests of givers, is equally well matched to the needs of recipients. Colleges and universities can answer that question better than corporations. They have been trying to communicate their feelings, and the points they raise deserve careful consideration by any corporation blueprinting an aid-to-education program for the 1970s.

The most urgent and consistent plea from the campus to the corporation is for more flexibility. Schools say they are especially in need of discretionary income, to be applied where and as they see fit. Data compiled for 1967-1968 show that only one-third of the voluntary financial aid going to colleges and universities came free of strings. Most gifts were earmarked for student aid, physical plant, research, or other specified purposes.

Useful and welcome as such aid may be, it remains that restricted gifts, unless they are based on close knowledge of the recipient's needs, reduce a school's freedom of action. Carried to extremes, such gifts may actually warp the functions of an educational institution by driving it into projects which happen to appeal to donors but which fall low on the priority list of the school. It is not the role or the wish of the corporation to do that.

There will always be those happy marriages where a university and corporation agree completely on the disposition of a grant or gift. There the question of restriction has no bearing. The gift may be earmarked, but its application is nonetheless educationally sound. As a general objective, considering the needs of the next decade and the pressures for change within educational institutions, corporations can help most by supporting programs developed by people close to the scene and qualified to rule on priorities. This can be done either through open-ended, discretionary gifts or through meetings in which donors and recipients jointly devise a strategy suitable for both.

In one college or university, the most pressing need may be for funds to support young faculty members. The school may have some particularly innovative instructors, but because they are young and have not had time to build their reputations, they may have more trouble than older men in attracting research and project support.

Alternatively, the need may be for new money to launch an interdepartmental center and graduate program not limited by the traditional boundaries of disciplines. This might be a uniquely attractive opportunity for corporate support, for one of the characteristics of research within the corporate sphere is a melding of disciplines into goal-oriented project groups. Corporations know from their own experience how productive this can be if it is wisely handled.

In another school, the greatest need may be for seed money to support germinal research projects. There is an inevitable risk of failure in first-phase research, and the more novel and daring the idea, the higher the risk. Yet this type of activity is particularly appropriate in a university and deserves support. If even a modest number of such projects succeed, new fields of exploration are created.

Seed money can have triple leverage. While it is helping to launch a new avenue for study, it can also provide the extra increment of support needed to keep a promising professor on the faculty. He in turn often brings in graduate students as junior investigators, adding an educational component to the project.

One university research foundation dispenses most of its grants this way, using seed money to put the hyphen between research-recruiting. Experience has shown that, after a year or two of such support in amounts of a few thousand dollars to each recipient, the investigators and projects prove themselves and begin to draw backing from fund sources such as government. These seed grants have provided the starting point for a number of doctoral dissertations, a fact that particulary pleases the foundation heads. As Peter Drucker has said, the best teaching is not done when a professor transmits what he knows to a student—a library can do that—but when the two of them set out together in search of something neither one knows. By encouraging such journeys, these gifts gain an importance far out of proportion to their size.

Needs change with time. Last year's top-line priority may have been land needed for expansion. The goal ahead may be a new library. An interim objective may be funds to underwrite programs of special help for disadvantaged students who come to the campus with inadequate secondary school background.

Circumstances intrude. For a good university struggling to become better, the prime need may be for reinforcement of graduate teaching. For a smaller college struggling to expand its liberal-arts base, a strengthened undergraduate science department may be acutely needed. State legislators and the large individual contributors, the angels every independent institution prays it will have, often have pet projects to which they wish to attach their names.

All this a collective argument in favor of corporate support with the fewest possible strings attached. That type of support, together with the intake from the alumni fund, represents for some schools the only discretionary money in sight.

There may be opportunities as well for corporations to contribute in nonmonetary ways. Some services they might provide could be of more value than their cash equivalent, at least in certain cases. As one example, companies can lend employees with credentials in specified academic fields to schools which need their expertise but cannot afford it on a continuing basis. Another route, and one that is perhaps worth more attention than it has received, is for corporations to make available specialized help in the business side of education. Many schools already are as expert as any corporation in such matters as accounting, control, administrative planning, construction, and financial analysis. Were this not the case, they would not be as strong as they are. But other colleges and universities are frank to admit that this is an area of real weakness, and that they would welcome a chance to have a corporate consultant. In corporations and colleges alike, there is the ever-present problem of allocating scarce resources and making sure you get your money's worth. This is an avenue that might repay exploration in the 1970s.

The corporate giver searches for some balance here, some rationale to guide his decisions. The services he can offer are limited; the grants and gifts, equally so. Knowing that aid to everyone makes a difference to no one, he looks for logic in the exclusion process.

Is it best to focus on colleges and universities that are already excellent, to keep them so? That is sometimes protested as "undemocratic." It smacks of elitism. As the song has it, "The rich get rich and the poor get children"—more children enrolling and no way to educate them. But a case can be made for this tactic. The schools of highest accomplishment create future faculty members for lesser known schools. They also conduct much of the best research, and provide many of the candidates for corporate employment. How can they be ignored?

Would it be better for corporations to leave those schools to their own devices, and give all their help to the underdogs? That case also has force. Unless more of these schools can rise to higher standards and broaden their educational offerings, there is little hope of meeting the goal of quality with quantity.

It has been suggested that the nation is trying to run too many colleges and universities, and that letting Darwin's natural selection take its toll among the weak would be a wiser policy. This has a chilling tone, especially in a nation that owes so much to colleges which in their infancy were pitifully weak, and were sustained only by the vision of a handful of citizens, often working in the name of the church. Had these colleges not survived, would the present educational establishment be nearly as good as it is today? Would it even exist?

That may be a lesson suggesting that corporations in the future would do well to look carefully at the newer and neediest schools. Among them may be found some novel and exciting educational ideas which these schools are free to pursue. They have nothing to lose by innovation, for there is no tradition to overturn. They are eager to establish themselves and, given exceptional leadership, some of them doubtless will. For such schools modest grants might make major differences.

By the same token, one can make a case for the older, liberal-arts colleges, some of which are richly endowed, most of which are not. Howard R. Bowen, in a newsletter to the alumni of Grinnell, the college he once headed, made an eloquent defense of the leadership role filled uniquely well by the distinguished small colleges dedicated to undergraduate liberal education. Few would quarrel with his contention that a shining light in education would be darkened if the Grinnells, the Carletons, and the Pomonas were to disappear.

Corporations are often said to suffer from tunnel vision. They look straight ahead and see the university science and engineering departments, and support these to enhance the corporation's technical position and recruiting opportunities. They do not always note the other departments which deal with political and social issues, conceivably the issues of greatest importance to the corporate future. There is a measure of truth in this statement. Perhaps corporations have defined their self-interest too narrowly.

A recent report on the social sciences prepared by a special commission of the National Science Board makes the case for the "soft sciences" especially well. As the report notes, corporations have every reason to interest themselves in research that strives to create better understanding of the political, social, and intellectual forces shaping the environment in which corporations operate. In the social sciences as well as the physical, corporate contributors can find a posture of enlightened self-interest.

The trouble with these arguments is that they are all so eminently sensible. America needs the large schools and the small; the public and the private; the new, innovative colleges feeling their way and the grand patriarchs mindful of their duties as leaders. The nation needs the sciences and the humanities, the hard knowledge to improve the physical world, and the wisdom to apply that knowledge wisely.

This being the case, no simple formula can be devised for corporate giving. Instead one must trust to a collection of individual judgments, based on a continuing dialogue between individual schools and corporations, with each defining its own objectives and both paying due regard to the critical mass problem occasioned when they spread themselves so thin that nothing happens effectively.

The educational system that has evolved in this country is a product of multiple influences and reflects multiple objectives. The private corporation is only one of these influences, and one of many beneficiaries. Like all other segments of society called upon to help support education, the corporation has a responsibility to match its increment of support to the needs of colleges and universities, and to its own role in society.

Agenda for the 1970s

ROGER M. BLOUGH

In any age one can be either pessimistic or optimistic about the future of the society in which one lives. Certainly it can be argued in these days that there are good grounds for pessimism. The war in Vietnam, the prolonged conflict in the Near East, poverty and hunger in large segments of the population in the United States, discrimination against minority groups, a declining tempo of operations in certain industries, and, last but not least, numerous problems in the area of higher education. These great national concerns may give some grounds for the belief that it is not "the best of times."

To those who are justly worried, however, about conflicts in Vietnam and the Near East, one can point to the fact that for twenty-five years the world has escaped the disaster of war involving the great powers. While American military commitments overseas are extensive, a major conflict that might involve the United States has somehow been avoided. There is even some hope that the present conflicts will be resolved.

While it is true some Americans face discrimination because of race and others are insufficiently clothed, housed, and fed, yet never before in the nation's history have so many enjoyed such a wide range of physical comforts as are produced by the industrial system today. Moreover, as evidenced by the preceding articles, industrial leaders are committed to correcting, insofar as it lies in their power, some of the inequities in the distribution of wealth and expanding opportunities for those who in the past have suffered discrimination. Thus there is evidence of equal weight that the present is not "the worst of times." In any event, it is the only time that is given Americans in which to work together to solve the problems that they face in common.

Nevertheless, the nation is told that the American system of higher education faces a crisis. After surveying the financial plight of the nonpublic institutions, *Fortune* published an article with the somber title: "Private Colleges—A Question of Survival." At about the same time a group of education writers produced a report based on interviews with five hundred college and university presidents, both public and private. The consensus of these administrators' comments was that "the money is not now in sight to meet the rising cost of higher education, to serve the growing numbers of bright, qualified students, and to pay for the myriad activities that Americans now demand of their colleges and universities." Individually and collectively, through their various educational associations, college and university presidents have loudly and frequently let it be known that they are looking to the federal government for a good deal more money in the future than has been coming from Washington. Moreover the Carnegie Commission on Higher Education reports that if the American nation is to get the "quality and equality" from higher education which it needs, then federal aid to colleges and universities must rise from an annual level in 1968 of $3.5 billion to $7 billion in 1970 and to $13 billion a year by 1976.

It is not surprising that institutions of higher education ask so much from the federal government. What is surprising, and disturbing, is that they expect so little from the private sector.

The corporation and the campus are interdependent. It is not enough to utter the truism which has become a cliché—that the corporation needs educated people to make a profit and the colleges need dollars to produce educated people. Corporate support of higher education contributes significantly to the long-range goals of a corporation, for business is not only concerned with producing goods and services at a profit today but also with the continuity of a profitable enterprise. If American business does not aid in the maintenance of liberal education as the bulwark of good government, it is not properly protecting the long-range interest of its stockholders, its employees, and its customers.

The problems in the area of higher education are not insurmountable. Indeed, most of them arise from the very fact that higher education in America is a success story of magnificent proportions. The number of students in American colleges and universities in relation to population, together with the rapidity of growth, is the principal cause of the financial difficulties in which these institutions find themselves. To be sure, shifting educational enrollment patterns, the increase in the number of graduate and professional students, more intensive work in the sciences, and inflation have increased the total cost of higher education. But above everything else, the fact that more students are provided opportunity for higher education is responsible for the increasing costs. This is not a problem but, in the terms that Edgar F. Kaiser uses elsewhere in this book, a challenge which the nation can face with pride.

Contributors to this book agree that in the decade ahead major business units and the leading universities will more and more assume responsibility for helping to remedy some of the critical social and environmental ills of society. The seriousness of urban problems calls for the best efforts of private business and higher education as well as those of government. All of the many demands on the corporate dollar do not change the obligation of business to support higher education.

When faced with the hard reality of giving or not giving, of supporting this or that institution or not supporting it, the analytical bent of businessmen evolves two lines of thinking; first, what are the facts; and, second, what are the alternatives. There is considerable agreement on the facts. Because of the age factors and the size of upcoming generations, before 1980 this country will about double its enrollment in institutions of higher learning. If this estimate is correct, it means doubling the number of faculty members, a vast number of new facilities, and newer types of facilities. It should also mean greater utilization of all facilities.

This remarkable change in the number of students will create all kinds of new situations, not the least of which are the sources for the wherewithal to provide housing, to grant scholarships, to find competent members of the faculty, to develop more efficient methods of instruction and plant utilization. There is what might be termed an availability problem.

Making what some would consider a conservative estimate, Howard R. Bowen says that requirements for higher education by 1980 will be at least $39 billion, nearly twice the $20.4 billion of expenditures in the academic year 1968-1969. This estimate was based on a constant dollar. If inflation continues at the rate of the past fifteen years, the 1980 budget may well be $50 billion. Dr. Bowen predicts that gift income to higher education would become a smaller percentage of the total, but asserts that its importance will increase. A private dollar will continue to be a vital part of educational finance, he said, because it is the most venturesome, flexible, unbureaucratic dollar that colleges and universities receive.

James F. Oates, Jr., former chairman of the Equitable Life Assurance Society of the United States, concluded that the view of a corporation as a strictly economic institution with no proper interest in the public welfare is no longer valid, if indeed it ever was. Mr. Oates is convinced that business should continue to try hard to maintain increased rates of giving to higher education in spite of the many demands for funds to undertake social programs.

In reference to the needs of the core city, Franklin H. Williams of Columbia University's Urban Center pointed out that ghetto students must have more scholarship aid, more supportive services, and even more subsidies than the average white student—and, to do the job properly, universities, particularly private ones, need more facilities, more faculty members and more financial aid. One may add that in some areas the disadvantaged white student also deserves more than usual consideration. Dr. Williams noted that hard-headed businessmen have begun to see that the corporation's health does in fact depend upon the community's health and that, therefore, it must make a socially conscious effort to help improve the quality of life in the society that surrounds it.

Dr. James M. Hester, president of New York University, agreed that universities have accepted new concepts of the community and that the particular focus of that recognition has been the institutions' obligation to the society and to the disadvantaged members of that society to provide new kinds of educational opportunities. This response to such a community need requires more adequate sources of support than presently exist. Business should help close this money gap. Business leaders should give thought, Dr. Hester said, to a new kind of valuation of their social investment—based, as many corporate leaders have suggested, upon a concern for the society in which business must operate and, on the other hand, upon the valuation of business by that society.

Edgar F. Kaiser saw good reason to believe the decade ahead will mark the real and strong beginning of a renaissance movement within the American system. This movement, however, will require renaissance men and women; and business will need more and more people who can properly be called "change-makers." Mr. Kaiser considered these change-makers as already being in short supply, and the prospects for reinforcing their numbers should give everyone cause for concern. He saw a necessity for a merger of ideas and purposes between business and education and asserted that business and education can be the cutting edge of change. Higher education needs not only outspoken public support and understanding by business leaders but financial support in substantially increased levels of corporate giving. The priorities of this new innovative partnership between business and education, according to Mr. Kaiser, call for top management's time and attention.

Joseph C. Wilson, chairman of the Xerox Corporation, addressed himself also to the need for leadership from the top. He said that the success of responsible corporate action in contributing positive solutions to public problems is directly proportionate to the commitment of its leadership. Mr. Wilson did not recommend any single organization or structure for business firms in conducting their public affairs. In his opinion, organization and structure are secondary to the ability and the willingness of the leaders at the top to foster a spirit of social responsibility which will penetrate throughout the ranks of an organization. It was his conviction that if those in private business are to retain or deserve to retain power, then business leaders must above all persuade people by actions, not speeches, that the exercise of that power is not going to be arbitrary, but instead will be responsible, perceptive, and humane. Dr. Howard R. Bowen, formerly president of a private college and of a public university and an economist by profession, took a look at all the items found in an institution's budget. He predicted rises in all costs, although some will not rise as fast in the 1970s as they did during the decade just ended. Faculty salaries, he believes, may not rise more than 3 per cent a year rather than 5 to 6 per cent a year, but he sees an offsetting increase in salaries for the nonprofessional staff which may be unionized on most campuses before the end of this decade.

What will be the role of business in providing voluntary support to higher education? William F. May, chairman of the American Can Company, said that the future changes in and challenges to sources of public and private support of higher education could have a particularly deleterious effect on less-prestigious schools which have fewer contacts, fewer friends, little research, and already rely heavily on government support and on a greater percentage of income from student charges. These conditions, he noted, are likely to place the cost of education out of the reach of less-affluent students and to deny educational opportunities to numerous young people.

Such prospects are not good for America, and they are not good for the enlightened self-interest of the business community, said Mr. May, and he suggested that as other public and private sources of income are obviously limited in their abilities to meet the new needs of education, it becomes necessary for the business community to fill the void.

Business needs to support education, he said, because it profits from the fruits of basic research and from the knowledge explosion. Any investment in higher education is an investment in the self-interest of the corporations. The colleges and universities are producing the young men and women who in the future will fill critical posts in corporations.

In terms of Dr. Bowen's predictions of a 100 per cent increase in the budget of higher education over the coming decade, Mr. May urged that corporations should plan to increase their rate of support by 10 per cent a year for the next ten years. To that recommendation I subscribe wholeheartedly.

Studies by the Council on Financial Aid to Education show that corporate support of higher education has increased, on the average, nearly 10 per cent a year over the last decade. Business should seriously consider doing as much in the decade ahead.

But to urge this is not enough, for, as many corporate executives appreciate, how the company gives can be just as important as how much it gives. Charles B. McCoy, president of du Pont, considered the criteria by which corporate gifts can be given leverage and even unique value. He noted that most corporations have focused their gifts in selected areas for a limited number of colleges and universities, according to their own corporate definitions. While there is merit in such a pluralistic structure, by which each business firm fashions its own link-pins to education, Mr. McCoy questioned whether this diversity, based on the needs and interests of givers, was equally well matched to the needs of recipients. He suggested that business could help most by supporting programs developed by people close to the scene and qualified to rule on priorities. This can be done either through open-ended discretionary gifts or through meetings at which donors and recipients jointly devise strategy suitable for both.

The education system that has evolved in this country is a product of multiple influences and reflects multiple objectives, said Mr. McCoy. The private corporation is only one of these influences, and one of many beneficiaries. Therefore, he believes, the corporation has a responsibility to match its increment of support to the needs of colleges and universities and to its own role in society.

One should not discuss higher education or the financial problems of the 2,500 senior and junior institutions, which today enroll some 7.5 million students and by 1980 will enroll over 11 million without saying something about that ubiquitous creature himself—the college student. We yet do not know enough about how people learn, how the mind works, why we think as we do, or our motivations, although we do hear a great deal, and hear it loudly, about what people say they want and should have—particularly students and those on the other side of the "generation gap." Viewing the youthful scene as a whole, should one not also gracefully concede—or, better still, proclaim—that today's student world is more vigorous, more competent, more aware, and more adaptable than was yours and mine? This new generation is undergoing a more rapid learning process enabling students, or is it better to say, forcing students to take part in the management processes at an earlier age than we did. It is engendering discontent, and that is disturbing. But it is also engendering individual and group capabilities for action—independent action—even though that action is too often less constructive than it should be.

In many ways, the restless campus is a product of the restless society—a society of rapid changes which are difficult to comprehend. A college dean recently commented that one aspect of this restlessness is a renewed concern on the part of the members of the community about the community. And with this concern goes a vigorous interest in having a greater say in the affairs of the community.

There is no reason to conclude that the colleges and universities cannot become more significant and "relevant," to use a much overworked word—relevant to this generation of students, which, as someone observed, has its own exhibitionists and dunces and worse, just as previous generations did. Corporate pocketbooks cannot be excused on the ground that the cause is unrewarding or even hopeless —the cause of providing new and transitional education from one generation to the next and of providing guidance based on acquired experience.

Languishing in the field of voluntary support is not the answer to marijuana and educational turbulence. Fiscal surgery is not the cure for student riots. Impoverization is not, so far as higher liberal education is concerned, a reasoned response to, at best, youthful exuberance and, at worst, wanton destruction of the so-called establishment.

One should not be distracted or deterred by headlines that popularize anxieties about student unrest. These students, with all their iconoclasm and eagerness, are needed. They, and only they, will be the managers of the world in which mankind will dwell in the future—the near future. They are the ones, come what may, who must be trained as the pragmatists, the doers.

In a realistic sense, corporate and personal understanding and support of our colleges are more than self-help; they are a profound expression of faith. And without that faith, we could be ringing an early curfew on the nation's progress.

There is no doubt, however, that some colleges and universities have been momentarily hurt by the actions of the militant minority. Although militant students represent only about 3 per cent of the total student body, it was feared that their actions might hurt the institutions in the area of badly needed financial support.

In 1969 a part of the nation's press sought to prove that student disruptions were causing a serious decline in gift support. From a few isolated examples of a drop in gifts, some concluded that this was a universal condition.

The exact opposite appears to be the case. The Council for Financial Aid to Education recently completed analyses of the data supplied by over one thousand colleges and universities which, among them, received about 85 per cent of all gift support from alumni and friends, corporations and foundations, and other private sources. The preliminary estimates make one optimistic that when the report of this annual survey is made public it will be revealed that gift support in the academic year 1968-1969 showed an encouraging rise. Corporate support is also expected to show a strong upward move.

Kingman Brewster, president of Yale University, earlier in this book commented on the restless campus, saying that there are some students on the campus who are unmotivated by the true purposes of the university. They are there only to achieve credentials, or to avoid the draft, or because their parents insist that they go when they do not want to. He sees an involuntary population which, being involuntary, sometimes seeks to manipulate the institution to alien ends.

Looking ahead, Mr. Brewster optimistically urged the nation to take counsel of its hopes rather than its fears. He looks forward to a time when the shadow of the draft is removed so that it ceases to affect the educational planning of students. He said that what we need is a realization that the university is not the right place for all people at all times. It is not the right place for all people some of the time, and it is not even the right place for some of the people all the time.

The president of Yale University observed that the great significance of the educational economy—like the great significance of the productive, commercial, financial, and industrial economy—lies not in its wealth but in the variety of initiatives. He believes that the seventies will demonstrate whether the reaction to the knowledge explosion is one which proliferates variety or one which reduces Americans to conformity—to the blueprint of a single political planner. The outcome, he believes, will probably depend more than anything else on the nature of the educational economy. If variety is the great hope for the seventies on the campus, said President Brewster, then the nation needs to cultivate a greater variety of sources of financial support. And on the financial side, as Dr. Bowen said so well, it is the private gift dollar that makes new ideas come alive, that permits exploratory innovations, that helps set standards, that provides the vital margin between excellence and routine mediocrity.

In economic terms, higher education—in fact the whole system of education—has been called one of our most important growth industries. "Education" is not listed by that name on the New York Stock Exchange, but many of the corporations which supply its physical needs do have their names there.

While recognizing the importance of tax-supported institutions, independent institutions need to be cherished, particularly the liberal arts colleges and universities. As enrollment at these institutions decrease as a per cent of the total students enrolled in higher education, they increase in inverse proportion in significance to society in general and to business in particular.

Then, too, our college presidents are caught in a continuous upward spiraling of operating costs, and they have deep concern for the future as they recognize that income, including tuition, must rise with costs if the institutions are to remain solvent.

Whether or not the financial problems are the most critical for college presidents at this moment may be debated, but these problems are not likely to evaporate very soon. If independent institutions are to remain strong centers of influence for liberalizing people and for humanizing our technological society, then they are going to need all of the financial help they can get. Some of this—perhaps much more of it—is going to come from the federal government, and we should face up to this. More of it will also come from the state governments. But with all that, the need for more private support grows daily greater.

In the latest survey of voluntary support published by the Council for Financial Aid to Education, and in all eight surveys it has undertaken, business corporations have been fourth among the sources of voluntary support. Corporations have provided about 15 per cent of the total, coming behind general welfare foundations with 25.5 per cent, nonalumni individuals with 23.4 per cent, and alumni with 21.3 per cent. However, the Research Division of the Council tells us that contributions from business corporations and alumni have not only been the most rapidly growing sources of support, they also have been the most stable sources of support. That is a good record by business, but one problem with this matter of voluntary support of higher education is that good is never good enough.

Although voluntary support will likely increase in absolute dollars during the next decade, it will probably decline as a per cent of the income for higher education. The least that corporate support can do is to increase at the rate of 10 per cent a year for the next ten years. It has grown at that rate over the past decade, and the corporate community can do no less in this decade.

The year 1980 may seem so far in the future that predictions about the state of higher education at that time will not disturb anyone. But 1980 is like the next marker along an interstate highway. If everyone joins in supporting academic excellence, then the carillon in the university tower will peal a joyous tune. If one turns away from this opportunity, thinking someone else will do it, then a word of caution is in order: "Ask not for whom the bell tolls. It tolls for thee."

Index